Start Your Own

PUBLIC RELATIONS BUSINESS

Additional titles in *Entrepreneur's* ***Startup Series***

Start Your Own

Arts and Crafts Business
Bar and Club
Bed & Breakfast
Business on eBay
Business Support Service
Car Wash
Child Care Service
Cleaning Service
Clothing Store
Coin-Operated Laundry
Consulting
e-Business
e-Learning Business
Event Planning Business
Executive Recruiting Service
Freight Brokerage Business
Gift Basket Service
Grant-Writing Business
Home Inspection Service
Import/Export Business
Information Consultant Business
Law Practice
Lawn Care Business
Mail Order Business
Medical Claims Billing Service
Personal Concierge Service
Personal Training Business
Pet-Sitting Business
Restaurant and Five Other Food Businesses
Self-Publishing Business
Seminar Production Business
Specialty Travel & Tour Business
Staffing Service
Successful Retail Business
Vending Business
Wedding Consultant Business
Wholesale Distribution Business

Entrepreneur MAGAZINE'S

startup

Start Your Own

PUBLIC RELATIONS BUSINESS

Your Step-by-Step Guide to Success

Entrepreneur Press and Jacquelyn Lynn

EP Entrepreneur. Press

Jere L. Calmes, Publisher
Managing Editor: Marla Markman
Cover Design: Beth Hansen-Winter
Production and Composition: Eliot House Productions

Library of Congress Cataloging-in-Publication Data

Lynn, Jacquelyn.
Start your own public relations business/by Entrepreneur Press and Jacquelyn Lynn.
p. cm. -- (Start your own)
ISBN-13: 978-1-59918-338-1
ISBN-10: 1-59918-338-2
1. Public relations firm—Management. 2. New business enterprises. I. Title. II. Series.
HD59.L96 2009
659.2068'1—dc22 2009001578

Printed in Canada

13 12 11 10 09 10 9 8 7 6 5 4 3 2 1

Contents

Preface

Public relations: Good or bad, every company has them. Savvy businesses manage their public relations—and because they are experts in whatever product or service they provide, not in public relations, they will turn to a public relations expert to assist with this process.

That's where public relations firms come in. Even companies large enough to have an internal public relations department often retain an outside firm as well.

Why do companies hire public relations firms? Many reasons:

- A strong, well-planned PR campaign can help a business in a variety of ways that go straight to the bottom line in the form of increased sales and profits.
- An outside agency will look at a company through fresh eyes, seeing public relations and promotional opportunities the owners and managers may miss.
- Using an outside agency allows a company to focus on its core business rather than spending time, energy, and money trying to develop expertise in a new area.
- An outside agency has the necessary skills, resources, and media contacts to develop and implement an effective PR campaign.

Public relations have always been critical to a company's success, but in the past, they were easier to manage. Back in the days when there were just three major television networks and few people had even heard of the internet much less thought about having a personal computer in their homes, managing the flow of information about companies and products was far less complicated than it is today—and than it will be in the future.

The explosion of media opportunities and the rapidly changing communications landscape are key drivers in the growth of the public relations industry. But there's much more to an effective public relations strategy than simply media, and companies are recognizing the need to be proactive when it comes to their image. According to the Council of Public Relations Firms, public relations spending will increase 11.8 percent to $4.26 billion from 2007 to 2011. The U.S. Department of Labor's Bureau of Labor Statistics projects that employment in the public relations field will increase faster than average through 2012.

It's important to stress that this is not a manual on how to "do PR," although we will discuss some specific strategies and techniques. This is a guide on how to set up your firm, how to choose your own market niche, how to acquire and maintain clients, and how to manage and grow your own company.

If you've been thinking about starting your own public relations firm, now is the time, and this book will walk you through the steps.

1

So What Is PR Anyway?

Public relations, or its abbreviation PR, is one of the more misused and even misunderstood terms in the business world—yet it's a critical element in a company's marketing strategy. If you're going to operate a PR firm, you need not only to understand what that means, you must also be able to communicate it to your clients.

Public relations is the relationship a company or organization has with its various publics, and those publics include customers and potential customers, employees, suppliers, investors, the media, and the general public. Typically in business, the term *public relations* is used to refer to the *management* of public relations. As a public relations professional, your job is to help your clients with that process.

The process of public relations is one of helping an organization tell its story and build goodwill with the public and those who influence the public, such as the media. The ultimate goal of PR is credibility.

The Role of a Public Relations Professional

Successful public relations practitioners are able to see themselves and their clients from a variety of perspectives, including through the eyes of every public the organization has. PR professionals are pivotal to the communications process,ensuring that messages are clear, honest, unambiguous, easily understood, and appropriate for the target audience.

Some PR firms are primarily implementers, taking direction from clients without being involved in strategic planning. This narrow role is short-sighted on the part of the client because a skilled PR professional can provide far more value if he or she is involved in the entire public relations process. This means becoming an integral part of the client's team, learning the client's operation and goals, helping to put together a strategy that will take the client from where it is now to where it wants to be, and then assembling the necessary elements to implement and monitor the strategy, and make adjustments along the way when circumstances dictate.

> **Bright Idea**
> One of the best ways to learn the public relations business is to get a job with an agency. You can get paid while you learn the ropes. It will also give you a great perspective on how to treat your own employees later on.

Ethics and Responsibility

The power of public relations brings with it a tremendous amount of responsibility. Perhaps PR professionals should follow the principle medical students are taught: first, do no harm. History is full of examples of PR professionals who, either intentionally or not, used the public trust they cultivated to convey a message that turned out to be wrong.

The "father of public relations," Edward L. Bernays (1892–1995), was the nephew of Sigmund Freud, which could be why he was able to incorporate an astute grasp of human behavior into his work for clients. His work should be studied by every PR professional today. Many of his campaigns are legendary, such as when he promoted Lucky Strike cigarettes during a time when women smoking in public was not acceptable by arranging for a parade of debutantes to march down Fifth Avenue while smoking. He is also credited with convincing America that a proper breakfast was more than just coffee and toast; it was bacon and eggs.

Today, of course, we know that smoking and excessive consumption of high-fat, high-cholesterol foods cause a long list of health problems. Certainly Bernays cannot be held responsible for what wasn't known about his clients' products, but his career did reflect a number of moral ambiguities. Most notable was his work for United Fruit Company in the early 1950s, when he used questionable tactics to generate support for an overthrow of a freely elected capitalistic Guatemalan government, which was replaced by one of the most despotic governments South America has ever known. That should give today's PR professionals pause.

Words of Wisdom

"If you once forfeit the confidence of your fellow citizens, you can never regain their respect and esteem. It is true that you may fool all of the people some of the time; you can even fool some of the people all of the time; but you can't fool all of the people all of the time."

—Abraham Lincoln

Don't try to separate your own values and ethics from those of your clients. Do your research, understand what you are being asked to do, and make sure you'll be able to sleep at night if you are successful.

PR and Publicity

Publicity, which is often a function of the public relations team, is gaining media coverage of a company, its products, and its people. Publicity helps spread information to gain public awareness of a product, person, service, cause, or organization, and can include mentions in print and online publications, on broadcast programming, and in other communication vehicles.

Public relations and publicity are not synonymous, but it's common for a PR campaign to include publicity. A client may say, "We need some PR," when in fact he means, "We need some positive publicity." It's your job to help him understand that he needs more than some favorable media exposure, and to show him how such exposure is part of an overall PR strategy.

It's Not Free Advertising

Publicity is not free advertising. Advertising is a paid message communicated through various media. Because it's paid for, the advertiser can control the content and placement of the advertisement. The organization seeking publicity can put its message out there but has no control over how—or even if—it will be reported in the media.

Your goal as a PR professional is to have your client's story accurately represented in the media, and this is not easy because media representatives are independent in their reporting. This is why the Council of Public Relations Firms differentiates between advertising and PR this way: "Advertising is purchased media; public relations is earned media."

Bill Stoller—whose website PublicityInsider.com offers a wealth of public relations and publicity information—defines publicity this way:

> At its core, publicity is the simple act of making a suggestion to a journalist that leads to the inclusion of a company or product in a story. Newspapers, magazines, TV programs, and radio shows have large amounts of space to fill and depend upon publicists to help provide story ideas, interview subjects, background information, and other material. For the most part, the act of making a suggestion to a journalist, when successful, will lead to one of two types of coverage: A story created from scratch built around the story "angle" you suggest (e.g., a feature story on your company; a story about a trend that you present to a journalist; an interview segment, etc.); or the inclusion of your product, company, or service in an already existing story (e.g., the reporter is already working on a story about your field and your contact with her results in your product being included in the piece).

Tools of the Trade

The standard public relations tools and techniques you might use include:

- *Entertainment product placement*. The placement of branded goods or services in a context usually devoid of advertising, such as movies, the story line of television shows, and news programs.

- *Podcast*. A collection of digital media files distributed over the internet for playback on personal computers and portable media players.
- *Press conference (or news conference)*. An event where journalists are invited to hear a presentation and then are usually offered the opportunity to ask questions.
- *Press kit (or media kit)*. A package of background materials detailing various aspects of an organization that is presented to members of the media. Press kits may be printed or available in an electronic format. Press kits typically contain some or all of the following: a fact sheet about the company or organization; a brief history; an annual report; a list of key personnel with brief biographical statements; a mission statement; copies of publicity materials, including press releases; photographs of personnel and/or products; listings of products and/or services; lists of awards and achievements; copies of editorial mentions of the organization.
- *Press release (or media release)*. An announcement of an event, information, or other newsworthy item issued to the press.
- *Product launch*. The introduction of a new product to the market.
- *Publication of information material*. Making information known to the public through off- or online means.
- *Satellite feed*. Broadcast material sent via a satellite.
- *Seminars*. Training events typically targeted to a company's customers or potential customers.
- *Special events*. Events designed to generate publicity and public interest.
- *Speeches*. Presentations that provide public and media exposure for the speaker and organization.
- *Video news release (or VNR)*. Video segments designed to look like news reports that are distributed to television newsrooms and incorporated into newscasts.
- *Webcast*. A live or recorded broadcast of an event over the internet.
- *Wire service distribution*. A news-gathering organization that distributes syndicated copy electronically; distribution by wire service is an alternative to traditional news release distribution methods of regular mail and fax.

2

A Day in the Life

So what's it like to run a public relations firm? One thing you can be sure of, no two days will ever be exactly the same. Situations and circumstances will change at a lightning pace. If you like peace, quiet, and routine, this is not the business for you.

Certainly there are some tasks you can expect to do on a daily basis. For example, every day you will spend time monitoring local and national media, reading and responding to e-mails, and returning calls. You'll also need to spend time on the administrative side of the business, making sure bills are paid, employees are supervised, and so on. And, of course, you should regularly market your services. Beyond those constants, who knows?

Any given day might see you working with a client to develop a sound public relations strategy, doing research, writing press materials, calling reporters, setting up press conferences, fielding media requests, helping clients deal with a crisis situation, and any of the countless other tasks that are the responsibility of a successful public relations firm.

One of the best ways to learn the public relations business is to get a job working for an established firm. You'll have the chance to develop your own skills and see the business side of the operation. You'll also be able to make connections that will further your career, whether or not you eventually strike out on your own. Just remember to always operate with the highest level of ethics and integrity, which means do the work you are paid for and respect any confidential information to which you may have access.

Words of Wisdom

"A public relations professional is part business manager, part sociologist, part cheerleader, part confessor, and part pit bull. The trick to being successful is to be prepared for anything. And you can always count on the fact that tomorrow will bring new and exciting challenges."

—Sara Harms,
Account Executive,
Waggener Edstrom, New York

The Perfect PR Professional

Though PR professionals need a broad range of skills, the most important are strong communications skills. You need to be able to express yourself both orally and in writing in a clear, concise way that is easy for others to quickly understand. You must also excel at the other half of communication, istening. Few things will lose you clients faster than if they feel you aren't listening. And reporters will quickly turn to other sources if you aren't accurately hearing and providing what they need.

Of course, creativity is also essential. This is not so much creativity in writing—you can hire copywriters for that—it's creativity in ideas, concepts, and strategies. It's looking at a situation and coming up with a plan that will set your clients apart in a positive way in the eyes of their various publics.

Successful PR professionals tend to be curious. They want to know and understand what's happening in their own world as well as in the worlds of their clients. They are also students of human behavior; they want to know what motivates people to do the things they do. This curiosity drives them to discover the information they need to serve their clients.

Beware!

The bigger your firm, the more time you're going to have to spend on administration and management, and the less time you'll be able to spend on serving your clients and doing actual public relations work. Be sure the type of firm you create will let you do the work you want to do.

You must be persistent. The guests you see every day on *The Oprah Winfrey Show* didn't get there with one casual telephone call to a producer. Except in rare situations, it takes repeated efforts over a period of time to see the results you want. And along with persistence, you need a thick skin. Don't take rejection personally. When a reporter says no to your pitch, it's not you—and it may not even always be your client. It's simply the circumstances, which could change at any time. You just have to stay in the game.

Finally, you must be happy with being the conduit to putting someone else in the spotlight. While some PR professionals may serve as spokespersons, s the PR person you are not the story—the story is your client.

Different Types of PR Firms

You have a lot of choices when it comes to deciding what type of public relations firm to open. In general, your choices are a traditional, full-service firm; a general boutique firm; or a specialized niche firm. Once you choose the type, you'll have to decide on the size, which could range from a one-person (you) operation to a company with hundreds or more employees.

A traditional, full-service firm will typically be large, often with multiple locations and a wide range of resources with which to serve clients. They generally operate on a monthly retainer fee and require contracts of six months or a year, which gives them time to get to know their clients and develop campaigns. Many full-service firms have specialty divisions targeting certain market segments. They may also have technology teams that can assist clients in areas such as social media, blogging, search engine optimization, and so on.

A boutique firm is a smaller operation that may have a physical office or function as a virtual team. Lower overhead costs mean boutique firms can charge lower fees,

Beware!

Expect the unexpected. Being in business is a lot like being married: You don't know what it's really like until you do it. No matter how long you're in the business or how many times you think you've seen it all, there will always be something to surprise you—an off-the-wall client, a bizarre project, erratic employees—and you might as well get used to it.

while often providing the same or sometimes better service than the traditional firm. Boutique firms may offer general public relations services or target specific market segments.

Specialized niche firms typically fall into the boutique category in terms of size and focus on a specialized niche. In the next chapter, you'll get a more detailed look at those niches.

Both boutique and niche firms may work with clients on a retainer basis using short- or long-term contracts or on a per-project basis.

Your Policies and Standards

Though you are not likely to ever have two days that are exactly alike, it's important that you maintain consistency and clarity in your policies and standards. You are not going to provide identical services for your clients, but your relationship with each of them needs to be governed by the same set of rules. Don't do for one what you won't do for another, and don't make exceptions—because if you do, someone will probably find out and you're likely to have an angry (or worse, former) client on your hands. And you won't be able to keep the fact that you are inconsistent a secret—word gets around.

You may want to consider establishing a code of ethics for your firm, even if you are a one-person operation. Write it down and show it to your clients and suppliers. This will let them know what your standards are and could help you avoid awkward situations.

Be Creative but Don't Spin

Spin is an often derogatory term that implies the use of manipulative or even deceptive tactics to present an event or situation in a heavily biased way. Certainly your job is to present your clients in the most positive light, regardless of the situation, but not at the expense of your own reputation or integrity. Thanks to the abundance of media outlets today, it's more difficult than ever to spin, but it's still possible.

A classic spin technique involves selectively presenting facts that support a particular position while ignoring those that contradict or oppose. Other spin techniques

Sample Code of Ethics

At the ABC Public Relations Firm, we commit to the following standards:

- To adhere to the highest standards of truth in all of our communications with our clients and the public.
- To provide honest and objective advice to our clients, and to act in our clients' best interest.
- To represent our clients with integrity and fairness.
- To avoid any deceptive practice.
- To act promptly to correct any error that we may inadvertently make.
- To restrict the giving or receiving of gifts and entertainment to those that are nominal, lawful, and occasional.
- To respect and preserve the intellectual property rights of our clients and of others.
- To respect the privacy of our present, former, and prospective clients and other organizations we serve.
- To compete with other public relations firms fairly and ethically.
- To avoid any real, potential, or perceived conflict of interest.

include using clever phrasing that assumes unproven truths, ambiguity, simply skirting the issue, or making unfair attacks on the opposing side. You often hear spin in relation to political or crisis situations.

Help your clients put the best face possible on bad news, but don't resort to spin.

3

What Do You Have to Offer?

One of the attractive things about the public relations profession is that it's not a one-size-fits-all industry. You'll find a variety of specialties and structures from which to choose.

In the last chapter, I talked about the basic types of PR firms. Now let's take a look at specialties within the industry and the services you can offer. Your firm can focus on one or several of these specialties.

In most, but not all, cases the more you narrow the focus of your services, the smaller your pool of potential clients becomes. Be sure that there is a sufficient amount of business out there so that you can meet your revenue targets by capturing a reasonable market share. With that said, there is a clear trend in the industry toward specialized PR practices and away from the giant, multifaceted communications firms, which means that there is plenty of opportunity for you to create the small, specialized PR firm of your dreams.

Public Relations Specialties

As you consider the type of firm you want to build, be aware of the tremendous scope of PR specialties available. Identifying a niche for your firm lets you establish yourself as an expert, build your own reputation, and increase client demand while you do what you enjoy. There are enough choices that you don't need to do a type of PR work that doesn't suit you. Let's take a look at the different areas in which you can specialize:

- *Book and author promotions.* Work exclusively with authors and speakers, promoting both of them personally and their books.
- *Broadcast public relations.* Produce video press kits, satellite media tours, radio news releases, radio media tours, and related content.
- *Business startup public relations.* Target companies in the startup stage.
- *Community relations.* Help clients manage their reputation and image at the local level.
- *Corporate positioning.* Help clients position their company and brands in the marketplace.
- *Crisis communications/crisis response.* Help clients prepare for and respond to the public relations side of a crisis situation.
- *Digital media relations.* Assist clients in understanding the rapidly changing digital media landscape and develop a strategy to maximize the opportunities it presents.
- *Environmental public relations.* Work with clients in environmentally and socially responsible businesses or with companies that need to improve or protect their environment image.
- *Franchise promotion.* Work with franchised companies to promote both the product and the franchise.

- *Grassroots PR.* Develop programs and strategies to target local, grassroots media on behalf of your clients with initiatives designed to spark a small group of influencers who will spread the word to a larger group.
- *Investor relations.* Specialize in information and disclosure management for public and private companies as they communicate with the investment community.
- *Issue management.* Apply various public relations strategies to the process of managing specific issues and aligning organizational activities and stakeholder expectations.

Beware!

Don't confuse a grassroots campaign with what is known as "astroturf," which is an artificial grassroots effort. In the PR world, astroturf refers to efforts by a political or commercial entity to create the impression of spontaneous grassroots behavior, when in fact it is carefully orchestrated and often deceptive.

- *Industrial (labor) relations.* Assist clients in using public relations strategies in influencing the relationship between management and workers, particularly workers represented by a union.
- *Marketing public relations.* The technique of using press releases targeted to consumers on the internet as a marketing tool.
- *Media relations.* Focus on the relationship a company develops with the media, including print, broadcast, and online, both mainstream and alternative.
- *Nonprofit public relations.* Serving a client base comprised of organizations that are not for-profit and applying the particular strategies they require.
- *Product launches.* Public relations strategies designed to support the launch of new products, including developing messages, preparing company representatives for public presentations, identifying third-party advocates, arranging speaking engagements, and media coverage.
- *Reputation management.* Tracking a client's actions along with reaction to those actions, then reacting to that information in an appropriate manner.
- *Special events.* Focusing on public relations for special events.
- *Specific industries.* Developing expertise in specific industry segments and targeting public relations services to those particular groups.

Choose a Blend That Works for You

There are many valid reasons for choosing a well-defined market niche. By targeting a specific market segment, you can tailor your service package and marketing efforts to meet that segment's needs. You'll also develop a reputation for expertise that attracts new clients.

Consider the different types of public relations specialties and then focus on the one (or ones) that will allow you to build the firm you envision. Think about what you enjoy doing—do you like working on strategy development and systematic campaigns or are you an "adrenaline junkie" who thrives on reacting to crises? Do you want to work with clients whose mission and goals you share? Do you want long-term relationships or would you prefer to move from project to project?

Bright Idea

Whether you choose to work in crisis PR, it's likely that at some point you'll have a client that's facing a crisis. If you don't have the skills to help in-house, develop a relationship in advance with a crisis PR specialist so you'll be prepared to help your client immediately if the need arises.

When Kate Kaemerle founded Entech Public Relations in Seattle, Washington, she combined her passions for the environment and technology to create a firm that specializes in high-technology public relations, digital public relations, environmental public relations, and green marketing. Jonathan Bernstein's firm, Bernstein Crisis Management, Inc., based in Sierra Madre, California, provides crisis management consulting to clients across the country and even some internationally. He doesn't offer marketing or promotion services—he helps his clients prevent crises, if possible, and deal with them if they happen. Rhonda Sanderson's Chicago-based firm, Sanderson & Associates, focuses on fulfilling the publicity needs of nationwide franchise systems as well as introducing new products for companies that want to develop a national profile. The expertise at Development Counsellors International, a firm founded by Ted Levine, headquartered in New York and operating across the United States and in several other countries, is economic development and travel.

Consider your own experience and expertise, as well as your interests. It's hard for a business to be successful if the owner isn't passionate about it, so choose a specialty or combination of specialties that you can get excited about and enjoy working in.

Public Relations Services

Once you've decided on your specialty area or areas, you'll need to think about exactly what services you want to provide for your clients. They could include some or all of the following, as well as other activities designed to enhance your clients' relationships with their publics:

- *Media releases.* Writing and distributing media (press) releases.

- *Media interviews.* Arranging for interviews for your clients with the print, broadcast, and online media.
- *Media kits/press kits.* Creating and assembling the information that goes into a media (press) kit.
- *Media relations.* Managing the relationship your clients have with the media.
- *Special promotions.* Planning and coordinating special promotions and events.
- *Guest columns.* Arranging for your clients to be featured as guest columnists in print and online publications.
- *Article placement.* Having articles either written by or mentioning your clients published in print and online publications.
- *Ghostwriting.* Writing articles, books, and other materials that will appear under your clients' bylines.
- *Letters to the editor/op-ed essays.* Writing and submitting letters to the editor and opinion essays to newspapers and magazines, commenting on previously published articles or on current events.

Technology, You, and Your Clients

Technology has made public relations a totally different ballgame than it was just a decade ago and than it will be a decade from now. You need to constantly pay attention to new technologies and be willing to change your services and strategies as necessary.

Consider that as recently as the mid-1990s, negative and unflattering news stories could appear and then disappear within a few days. Today, bloggers and sites such as YouTube give such news items a virtually indefinite life. Your clients cannot take the attitude of "ignore it and it will go away" to a negative issue because, thanks to the internet, "it" will never go away. The impact of technology and the internet is discussed further in Chapter 6, but the point is that some strategies that worked in the past will not work today and some strategies that are working now may not work in the future.

Invest time in study and research so that you don't get blindsided by a technological innovation. You don't have to stay at the leading edge, because you don't know what will have staying power, but you need to stay ahead of the biggest part of the crowd.

- *Marketing PR.* Using press releases as marketing tools.
- *Seminars and workshops.* Assisting your clients in developing seminars and workshops that will enhance their public image and then promoting those events.
- *Speaking engagements.* Arranging for your clients to speak to appropriate groups.
- *Press conferences.* Arranging press conferences, including setting up the facility, inviting the media, and assisting clients in the presentation.
- *Market research.* Doing the necessary research to assist clients in determining the appropriate public relations strategy.
- *Contact lists.* Developing appropriate contact/media lists for individual clients. (These lists may or may not be shared with the client.)
- *Reputation monitoring.* Monitoring print, broadcast, and online media, including blogs, social media, and discussion boards, for mentions of your client, and reporting your findings.
- *Crisis response.* Assisting clients with appropriate response when a crisis occurs.
- *Media training.* Preparing clients for media interviews.
- *Other training.* Providing clients with training as necessary to protect and maximize their public relations efforts.

Seeing the Big Picture

It's possible a small-business client will hire you to simply write a press release or another very specific task in the PR process. The best way for you to serve such a client is to help them see the big picture of PR and how your services can be blended with corporate communications, advertising, and marketing to achieve strategic goals. To do this, you must not only understand your business of PR but business in general and your client's business in particular.

"Imagine a world in which you can tell clients ahead of time, through research and an analysis of the best practices, which communication vehicles would be most likely to enhance the firm's reputation, make employees happy, and increase stock price to its fullest potential," said Paul A. Argenti, Professor of Corporate Communication at the Tuck School of Business at Dartmouth. "If you can imagine that, you can probably also imagine a world in which PR firms would no longer be hired just to implement strategy, but also to develop the right strategies to have the greatest impact on constituencies. But to do this, you will need to hire people with a greater understanding of business and you will have to reward them accordingly. I have always thought that PR should come out of the cold and become part of the club. The business elite come from business schools today and PR people need to realize that they must not only be excellent at communication but also understand finance, marketing, operations, etc."

Timing Is Everything—Most of the Time

As a PR professional, you'll offer guidance to your clients in terms of the timing of their various communications and events. For example, if your client wants to hold a big special event and hopes to attract media attention, you need to find out if anything else is scheduled for that date and time that would divide or dilute possible coverage. Certainly you can't control unexpected news events, but you should be aware of what's planned.

You also need to time your press releases for optimal effectiveness, considering both the reporters and your ultimate audience. In general, radio cutoff is up to an hour before "drive time;" television cutoff is up to an hour before newscasts; daily newspaper cutoffs are up to three hours before printing but stories are generated a day or more prior to publication; weekly publication cutoffs are usually two days prior to printing; monthlies can be weeks or even a month in advance.

There may be situations when you are obligated to issue a press release but you'd really prefer for it to get little, if any, attention. In general, those releases should go out toward the end of the week when reporters are tired and focused on their own weekend rather than your news.

While your press release may get overshadowed by other news, don't depend on a strategy of hiding your own bad news behind more spectacular events. One of the most famous and repugnant incidents of using a disaster to hide negative information occurred on September 11, 2001. Less than two hours after both of the World Trade Center towers and the Pentagon had been attacked, Jo Moore, a press officer with the British government, sent this e-mail to the press office of her department: "It's now a very good day to get out anything we want to bury. Councillors' expenses?" When the e-mail was leaked nearly a month later, Moore apologized and eventually resigned. The phrase "a good day to bury bad news" has since been used to describe the strategy of attempting to hide a news item under a more publicized issue.

4

Who Are Your Clients and How Do You Sign Them Up?

Once you've decided on the type of services your firm will specialize in and the services you want to provide, you need to identify your potential clients. Create a picture of the type of company that needs what you're going to offer. What size is the company? What business is it in? What kind of marketing and public relations budget does it have? What sort of special PR challenges does it have?

With a clear image of your prospective clients, you'll know how to reach out to them. Of course, when you happen across a potential client that doesn't exactly fit your profile, don't pass it by—consider whether or not you could make a relationship work. Getting too far outside your target market will probably not work for either you or the client, but you can push your boundaries somewhat and still be successful.

It's important that you maintain a broad client base. You need enough clients so that losing one—or even several—is not devastating. Never allow a single client to control so much of your revenue that you would have trouble operating if you lost that client.

Marketing Your Firm

Market your PR firm in the same ways most professional services are marketed: through networking, referrals, possibly advertising, direct selling, and, of course, public relations.

You'll likely get most of your business through referrals and networking. Advertising might raise awareness of your company, but public relations agencies are rarely chosen on the basis of paid ads. You can usually get more for your money by using other marketing strategies. Once you identify a potential client, you'll need to use sales skills to close the deal. And be sure that you are always using your public relations skills to promote your own business as well as your clients.

Bright Idea

Your satisfied clients are your best marketing tool. Most will be happy to endorse you and allow you to use their name and recommendation in your marketing materials—after all, it's one more place they can get their own name out in front of people.

Your Web Presence

In today's business environment, a great website is absolutely essential for any business—and especially for a public relations business that will likely be advising clients on how to enhance their online image. A professionally-designed website is a worthwhile investment. Chapter 6 discusses the impact of the internet on public relations. Apply that information to your own business as well as to your clients.

Seminars and Workshops

A great way to promote your firm and establish yourself as an expert in your specialty is to offer seminars and workshops. You can do these for free or for a nominal cost. They can be held in a classroom situation or via webinar (online) or teleseminar (telephone). Focus on some of the services you provide or on some of the special PR challenges companies in your target market are likely to face.

While it may sound self-defeating to offer to teach people to do for themselves what you'd like to do for them for a fee, it isn't. Many people will listen to your advice, respect your knowledge and expertise, realize the work is too challenging for them to do in-house, and call you to do it for them—and, of course, pay you well for your efforts. Or they may refer someone else to you.

> Tip...
>
> **Smart Tip**
>
> Ask every new client and potential clients how they found out about you. Make a note of where they heard about you and what kind of business they represent. This will let you know how well your various marketing efforts are working. You can then decide to increase certain programs and eliminate those that either aren't working or are attracting a type of business you don't want.

Trade Shows

Business-to-business trade shows could be a tremendous marketing and networking opportunity for you. You don't need to exhibit; especially when you're just getting started, the cost of a trade show exhibit may be beyond your budget. Use the shows as a networking opportunity as well as a chance for you to educate yourself on companies and industries. Just remember that exhibitors pay a substantial amount of money to set up at a show, and they're there to get business, not buy services. Don't waste their time on the exhibit floor if you're not a prospect for them; make your own sales contact later.

Many shows have refreshment areas and scheduled seminars and networking events where you can mix and mingle with exhibitors and other attendees. This is a good opportunity to acquire business cards of potential clients for later follow-up. However, don't just stuff the cards into your pocket; when you can, make a few notes on the card to remind yourself of who the person was and whether or not they indicated any interest in your services. After the show, use the cards you collected as sales leads.

Don't bother to take brochures to a show if you're not exhibiting—just take plenty of business cards. Put your own business cards in your left pocket and reserve your right pocket for the cards you collect. That way you won't risk accidentally giving away someone else's card.

Wear business clothes to trade shows. Just because the event is held at a resort doesn't mean you should dress like you're on vacation. And no matter how creative you are when it comes to organizing campaigns, public relations is a serious business and your appearance needs to reflect that. But remember that at trade shows, you'll likely be on your feet all day, so wear comfortable shoes. Don't chew gum or smoke, and avoid alcohol even at cocktail parties—you're there to make a good impression and get new business, not to play.

Pitching Clients

In most cases, your client pitch will involve a series of telephone calls, meetings, a written proposal, and a formal presentation. Your initial contacts will be primarily fact-finding in nature because you'll need to gather sufficient information to make an adequate proposal.

Your proposal document itself should include:

- An overview of the client's company and needs
- The solutions you can provide
- The results you anticipate
- The resources you bring to the process (your skills and experience, the experience of your team, your network, and so on)
- Credibility-builders, such as a list of successful campaigns and recommendations of other clients
- Fees and other costs
- A signature page

Your proposal should provide a clear overview of what you do and how you operate without giving too many specifics. Don't make your proposals so detailed that companies can take the information and implement your plan without you. Remember that a detailed PR plan

Bright Idea

When you give your business card to someone, give them two—one to keep, and one to share. It's much easier for someone to make a referral if they can just pass your card along. Wherever you are, whether it's a business or social situation, offer your card when you are introduced. This ensures people know your name, what you do, and how to reach you—and will remember.

is part of your product; don't share too much of it until you have a contract signed and a check in hand.

Proofread your proposals carefully. If there are typos in your proposal, why should a client think you can prepare error-free news releases? And while it's natural that you'll develop templates and use material from one proposal in another, check it carefully to make sure that it's not personalized for the wrong client.

Your proposal can serve as the outline for your presentation. You can also create a modified version as a PowerPoint presentation to add some visual pizzazz to the process.

Sales and Negotiation Skills

Public relations involve the buying and selling of an intangible service, and it is not always easy to measure results, which makes this a strong relationship business. You'll use face-to-face and telephone sales skills both as you acquire new clients and as you implement their public relations plans.

Don't let the word "selling" scare you. Most of the world's top sales professionals will tell you they hate "selling." What they mean is, they hate the vision of the slick,

Whom Should You Associate With?

Membership in associations is a key networking tool for PR firms. You should be a member of PR industry professional organizations so that you stay current on issues affecting your business. Associations such as the Public Relations Society of America (PRSA) include members from various industries, government, and nonprofits as well as PR firms. It's common for company PR staffers to have business handled by outside firms. Many national associations have state and local chapters; your local business journal should publicize their meetings—if not, get in touch with the national office to find out about a local chapter.

You should also belong to the associations your clients and prospective clients belong to. This helps you increase your own industry knowledge and provides you with a wealth of networking opportunities. For example, Rhonda Sanderson of Sanderson & Associates specializes in public relations for franchises, so she is actively involved in organizations such as the International Franchise Association.

fast-talking character on the used car lot or the door-to-door peddler who wedges a foot in the door and won't leave until you buy. But that's not "selling" in the professional sense of the word.

When you sell as a public relations professional, you convince prospective clients that you have the capabilities to help them with their PR needs better than any other firm—and if you don't believe that, you don't need to start a PR business. You are not going to browbeat a client into signing on with you, nor are you going to manipulate them into buying services they don't need. You're going to provide the best professional PR service that meets their needs at a fair rate, and communicating that is a major part of the sales process. You will also use selling skills in your relationships with the media and with the other publics you'll be dealing with. If you've never taken any professional sales training, it's a worthwhile investment.

Qualifying Prospects

The first step of the sales process is qualifying the prospect, which is sales training jargon for determining how much business the potential client has and who makes the decision as to what firm is going to get it.

This is not as hard as it seems. It really involves asking a few simple questions. If you networked your way into the company, you probably have a pretty good idea of the answers. When you make a contact with a prospective client, just ask questions such as, "Who in your firm is responsible for public relations?" and "Who makes the decision on which PR firm to retain?"

While it's critical to identify the real decision maker, which may be an individual or a team, you shouldn't ignore the decision influencers. These are the people who are in a position to influence the decision-making process and could be telephone operators, receptionists, administrative workers, sales representatives, marketing personnel, and even high-ranking corporate officers.

Think about this: You and another PR firm are competing for a particular account. The company's owner will make the final decision with input from the senior management team.

Beware!

Be careful that you don't patronize or insult the support staff of your clients or prospective clients. Keep in mind that these people may not only influence the decision-making process, but also they may eventually be promoted to decision-making positions—either with that company or with another. So treat them with respect, be concerned about their needs, and nurture a professional relationship with them.

You and the other firm have similar resources, and while your ideas aren't identical, you could both do an effective job. But the other firm took the time to talk to the marketing director's assistant as part of its proposal preparation process. So when the marketing director asks the assistant for input before making a final recommendation to the owner, which firm will have the edge in the assistant's mind? The firm that clearly cares about her opinions and needs.

This doesn't mean you need to wine and dine every assistant or send flowers and candy to all the receptionists in the hopes that they'll put in a good word for you. What it means is that you should demonstrate that you respect their role in the process and that you want to be sure you identify and meet their needs.

Determining Needs

Remember, every organization has public relations—they just have different publics and manage the relationships with those publics differently. Before you start telling a prospective client what you can do for them, find out what they need. It's a waste of your time and theirs for you to do this any other way.

To find out a company's needs, simply ask. "Before I tell you about our services, I'd like to ask you a few questions and find out exactly what you need." Then ask questions about the company's business, marketing strategy, and challenges that you may be able to assist with. Most of the time, you'll get plenty of information. Have a notebook handy and take notes; don't count on being able to accurately remember all the details you'll learn. Jot down any ideas you might have for strategies as you're listening as well—this will be very helpful when you put together your proposal.

Part of determining needs includes learning about the company's decision-making process. Again, all you need to do is ask: "Who will make the final decision and how will that process be handled?" Will you need to make a written proposal? A detailed face-to-face presentation? Are other firms being considered? Will the company prepare a request for proposal (RFP) detailing what services are required?

Most companies will be upfront about what they're looking for and the procedures they're

Bright Idea

Thanks to the internet, it's easier than ever to find out about your competition. Before you get started, study the websites of other public relations firms in your geographical area as well as in the specialties on which you plan to focus. Then set aside some time at least once a month for browsing the internet looking for website updates or sites of new companies.

going to follow. If they're not, it's a red flag—if they're not open and honest with you from the very beginning of your relationship, they may be difficult to work with later on.

Features and Benefits

You've probably heard the sales training phrase "sell the sizzle, not the steak." What this means is you need to understand the difference between features and benefits—and focus on the benefits.

A feature is an aspect of the service you provide; the benefit is what the customer gains from that aspect. For example, the fact that you're on a first-name basis with several producers who book guests for the top-rated cable business shows is a feature. That you can get your clients on those shows and that the exposure will enhance their public image and lead to great sales is a benefit. That you're a great writer and know how to use keywords in press releases to appeal to search engines is a feature. That you can use press releases to increase your clients' internet visibility is a benefit.

The Real Issue Behind Objections

Another long-time sales training phrase is "handling objections." That sounds much more frightening than it really is.

In most professional sales situations, an "objection" comes in the form of a question. Whether it's a question or a statement, it's usually a request for more information. For example, when a potential client says things such as "Our customers don't buy online, so why should we bother issuing online press releases?" or "We prefer not to publicize our community service efforts," you have a great opportunity to demonstrate your knowledge and explain what the client will gain by using your services and following your advice.

When you explain any part of your services, ask questions that will confirm that the client understands and agrees with the value you provide. A sales presentation should never be a lecture; it's a dialog.

> **Bright Idea**
> Submit your work for consideration in various industry awards programs at the local, regional, and national levels. In addition to bragging rights, winning industry awards increases your visibility and credibility among your clients and potential clients.

Business Entertaining

Entertaining clients and prospective clients over a meal is a great opportunity to showcase your social skills and level of sophistication. It's also a chance to get to know your clients in a more relaxed atmosphere.

Some general issues to keep in mind about business entertaining include:

- Business entertainment takes a variety of forms, most commonly lunch or dinner, but it could be breakfast, coffee, a sports event, or other community event.
- The location or event should be high quality but not so extravagant that it appears as though you are attempting to "buy" the business.
- Generally, the person who issues the invitation will pay, but you should always be prepared to pick up a check even when your client is the one who suggests going out.
- To reduce the risk of potentially embarrassing situations, keep alcohol consumption to a minimum or avoid it altogether.
- Never invite a client to a restaurant you haven't already been to and are confident about.
- Check with your accountant to find out what records you need to keep to deduct your business entertainment expenses on your tax return.

Ask for the Business

One of the most difficult parts of a sales call for most people is the close—but it shouldn't be. If you've been paying attention and identified your prospect's needs and determined that you can satisfy them, if you've focused on benefits rather than features, then asking the prospect to make that final commitment should be the natural evolution of the sales process.

Here's one approach that works well: when your presentation is complete and all of the prospect's questions are answered, ask what internal procedure the client would have to follow so that you could begin your work. This is a simple matter of asking: "Which department would you like me to begin working with first so I can get the information I need to put together a master plan for you?" When the prospect answers the question—perhaps with something like, "You will need to interview our sales manager to find out the biggest challenges our salespeople are facing"—ask if the sales manager can step into the meeting so you can answer any questions the person might have. Following that, getting the contract signed will be a comfortable formality.

If the prospect resists, find out why. Say: "We've agreed that a strong public relations campaign will increase your sales and my firm is in a position to get started on developing and implementing that campaign right away. Is there any reason why we shouldn't bring the sales manager in at this point?"

Prospects rarely say no without some sort of an explanation—an objection—that you'll have a chance to overcome. And even if you don't get the business—and you won't get it all—at least you'll know why.

Sample Contract

Agreement for Public Relations Work

This agreement is between [name of PR firm] and [name of client] for public relations work [PR firm] will undertake in order to [briefly describe the goal of the work].

The work will begin on [commencement date] and will continue on a monthly basis until such time as this agreement is terminated by either party. The scope of work is described in Attachment A. Deliverables related to the scope of work are described in Attachment B.

If [Client] requests [PR firm] to complete additional activities not described in Attachment A or to produce deliverables not described in Attachment B, [PR firm] will propose an addendum to this agreement and additional fees may apply.

[PR firm] will assign an account manager who will be [Client's] primary contact and will be responsible for the implementation of work covered by this agreement. [Client] will appoint a primary contact who will work with the account manager and coordinate all communications with [PR firm].

In exchange for the services described in Attachment A, [Client] will compensate [PR firm] a monthly fee of $XX. The first month's fee is due on signing of this agreement, and then due on the ____ day of each month thereafter. In addition, client agrees to reimburse [PR firm] for expenses listed in Attachment A within 30 days of receiving an invoice with documentation for said expenses. [PR firm] will secure advanced approval from [Client] for any single expense not originally agreed upon.

All design material, media events, and any other public relations or marketing initiatives will require approval from [Client] before printing or scheduling. If printing errors occur after [Client] approves a proof that contained errors, reprinting is the financial responsibility of [Client]. If errors caused by [PR firm] or a contractor of [PR firm] that did not have [Client] approval occur, corrections including reprinting and redistributing will be the financial responsibility of [PR firm].

The initial duration of this agreement is for six months. Should [Client] elect to terminate this agreement without cause on the part of [PR firm] during this initial period, [Client] will pay fifty (50) percent of the balance remaining. After the initial period, either party may terminate this agreement without cause with 30 days' written notice. If [PR firm] fails to deliver on the terms of the agreement, [PR firm] would be at fault and subject to termination without financial compensation.

Sample Contract, continued

[Client] agrees to work with [PR firm] to complete the activities and deliverables described in Attachments A and B by providing requested information and feedback within a timely manner. If delays on the part of [Client] staff or representatives cause additional work or delays, additional fees may apply.

[PR firm] shall treat as confidential all information relating to the services described in Attachment A, except where the revelation of such information is within the scope of work. [PR firm] shall not, without prior consent of [Client], use or disclose information deemed confidential to persons not authorized by [Client] to receive same.

All information, property, and records pertaining to [Client] are and shall remain the property of [Client].

[PR firm], its designees, and their respective directors, officers, partners, employees, attorneys and agents, shall be indemnified, reimbursed, held harmless, and defended from and against any and all claims, demands, causes of action, liabilities, losses, and expenses (including, without limitation, the disbursements, expenses, and fees of their respective attorneys) that may be imposed upon, incurred by, or asserted against any of them, or any of their respective directors, officers, partners, employees, attorneys, or agents, arising out of or related directly or indirectly to this Agreement. This paragraph, insofar as it applies to work undertaken while this agreement is in effect, shall survive the termination of this agreement.

This agreement along with Attachments A and B constitutes the full agreement between the parties.

Both parties signify their acceptance of the terms described herein by affixing their signatures below.

PR Firm: ______________________	Client: ______________________
Address: ______________________	Address: ______________________
______________________	______________________
(signature) date	(signature) date
Name, Title: ______________________	Name, Title: ______________________

Sample Contract, continued

Attachment A: Scope of Work

Under the terms of the attached agreement with [Client], [PR firm] will complete the following scope of work:

[describe scope of work]

____

____

____

____

____

____

____

____

Attachment B: Deliverables

As part of the completion of the scope of work described in Attachment A, [PR firm] will deliver the following items to [Client]:

[list deliverables]

____

____

____

____

____

____

____

5

Client Relations

Your goal should be to develop long-term relationships with your clients so that you can become an integral part of their team—even if your business model is designed around services such as crisis response or even short-term project PR. Let them know that your first priority is their success. In addition to keeping them on your client rolls, this will increase the referrals they make to you and contribute to your firm's growth.

Know Your Clients

You should know your clients' businesses as well as you know your own. It's impossible to effectively manage public relations for a company if you don't understand what it does or how it operates. A client that won't take the time to educate its PR firm is dooming the effort to failure. Ask for plant tours. Visit retail outlets. Get product samples and actually use them if possible. Talk with employees at all levels in all departments. Interview customers. Do internet searches to find out what's being said about the company and confirm what's accurate and what's not.

Set up comprehensive files and don't rely solely on your memory for retaining and managing this information. Sometimes you may simply not be able to recall a particular detail you need, and you should be able to find it out without going to your client. If you have a change in staff, you want to be able to bring the new person up to speed on the client before making an introduction; complete files will make this possible.

Maintain key client information in an easily accessible electronic database that includes the company name, location(s), contacts, telephone numbers, e-mail addresses, other pertinent information, and detailed project logs. These records should be constantly updated. At any given point, you should be able to look at a client's file and know everything you need to know about the company. You should also always be able to quickly summarize what you've done for the client and the results the work produced.

Your Role in the Process

Be very clear about your role in your clients' public relations process from day one. Tell your clients that if they're looking for a "yes person," they need to look elsewhere. A key part of your job is to provide objective advice and recommendations, so make it known that when you think the client is wrong, you'll speak up vigorously. You are also committed to pushing your clients to take whatever action is necessary to

> Tip...
>
> **Smart Tip**
>
> You don't have to share your media list with your clients; you've worked hard to build it, and you are under no obligation to give it away.

meet their goals. Let them know you'll nag, prod, pester, and generally do what it takes to keep things moving.

Blend Public Relations with Your Clients' Sales and Marketing Efforts

Certainly there is a difference between public relations, sales and marketing, and even operations and production, but those respective functions will be more powerful if they are working in concert. Make it a practice to encourage all of the key functions in your clients' organizations to participate in the public relations process. For example, let's say your client has made a major investment in energy-saving equipment. Your client may simply be thinking of the long-term savings involved; it's your job to know about the purchase and let your client know that it can have a PR benefit.

On the other side of the coin, teach your clients to take advantage of what you do. When a company is mentioned in a news article, for instance, make sure it puts a link on its website, includes the article in its press kits, and its sales representatives mention the article on their calls. Help companies maximize the impact of positive publicity.

A great PR strategy is to tie your clients into a national event. While this is generally your responsibility, it will be helpful if your clients understand it and can let you know when a news event is happening so that you don't miss it. For example, let's say your client is an engineering firm in Georgia. A building under construction collapses in Arizona, resulting in the death of several workers and a bystander. Because of the degree of tragedy, that incident in Arizona is likely to be covered by Georgia media, both broadcast and print. Reach out to local reporters offering your client as an expert source who can give their stories a local angle, including "can it happen here?" Teach your clients that if they become aware of any news situation for which they can be a positive resource, you are to be contacted immediately.

Media Training for Your Clients

A key part of a PR firm's job is to get media coverage for their clients—and that usually means the clients will participate in interviews. It's not enough to simply set up the interview—be sure your client is able to handle the process. At the very least, provide your client with guidelines for how to conduct the interview. Use the Interview Guide on page 42.

Even better is to conduct more in-depth training with your clients. Role-play interviews so your clients can practice their responses. Record the role playing on video and critique it, then do it again so your clients can correct mistakes. Consider bringing in an image consultant to assist your clients with dress, hair, makeup, mannerisms, and other physical presence issues.

You may also want to review your clients' media policies. If they don't have a policy, help them create one. The larger the company, the more important it is to have a clearly stated media policy so that everyone knows how media inquiries should be handled and who is allowed to speak publicly on behalf of the company. See the Sample Media Policy on page 45.

Tip...

Smart Tip

Always try to see things from your client's point of view, no matter how unreasonable or demanding they seem. Remember that what you see as nagging, repetitive phone calls could be your client's way of expressing anxiety, or that you may end up on the receiving end of a flare of temper that isn't actually directed to you at all. You don't have to take abuse, but be as understanding as possible.

Don't Let Your Clients Make Mistakes

When your client wants to do something that you know would be ineffective or even damaging, you need to do everything you can to stop it. For example, don't let your clients spam the media with press releases—or have you do it for them (that not only hurts your client, it also hurts your reputation). If your client isn't happy with an article but it contains no factual errors, don't let him complain to either the reporter or the editor. Explain that a complaint not only isn't going to change what was published, but also won't endear him to the reporter, which could affect what, or even if, the reporter writes about him in the future.

Remember that you are the public relations professional and your clients are paying you for you expertise and judgment. You may have to periodically remind your clients of this, especially when you are dealing with spontaneous entrepreneurial types who like to make decisions, take quick action, and be in control. Be prepared to explain the consequences of a mistake so that your client can see the wisdom in following your advice.

The No-Charge Invoice

Your contracts should clearly spell out what you're going to do for your clients and how you will be compensated. Even so, there will be times when you choose to do work for your clients for which you will not charge. Consider letting them know what you've done by issuing a no-charge invoice—an invoice that details the work and its value, and indicates that there is no charge.

You can include no-charge items on your regular invoice or create a separate document. In addition to letting your clients clearly see the bonuses they've received, this is a great way for you to track the work you do for which you aren't billing. When it's time to renegotiate a client's contract, review the no-charge work and keep that in mind as you work out the new details.

Dealing with Difficult Clients

Not all clients are created equal, and some are more difficult to work with than others. Some clients will be great to work with, while others will be extremely demanding, wanting you to be available at all hours, and expecting unrealistic results.

The first step in dealing with difficult clients is to set your boundaries and stick to them. Know how much you're willing to take and what you're going to do if a client exceeds your limits.

Some difficult clients simply need training. You need to explain to them how you work and how things have to be for you to get your job done—the job that you are doing for them as well as the work you are doing for other clients. If training isn't enough, you may need to restructure your contract to accommodate the client's demands and be compensated for additional

Tip...

Smart Tip

Meeting deadlines is critical to successful public relations campaigns. As you're putting together project timelines with your clients, be sure you make this very clear. Missed deadlines generally mean missed opportunities—and less-than-desirable results.

work. Some people will push you to do more until it's going to cost them more, and then they back off. Remember that you teach other people how to treat you, so if you allow abuse, it will likely keep happening.

Keep detailed records of your dealings with difficult clients so you have documentation if necessary. Such records are also useful when you evaluate whether or not the client is worth the pain and trouble.

Above all, keep your sense of humor and be honest and fair in all your client dealings.

When You Have to Fire that Troublesome Client

Not all client relationships are worth saving. Sometimes you just have to walk away, but you need to do that in a calm, professional way. Your contracts should include a termination clause that can be used by both you and your clients. The clause could be as simple as, "This contract may be terminated without cause with 30 days' written notice." (Or you may want to include some termination penalties. That depends on the nature of the work you're doing for the client as well as the fee structure.)

> **Bright Idea**
> Check out the Institute for Public Relations website at instituteforpr.org for information on how to measure results from public relations efforts.

When it's time to end a client relationship, keep your written notification simple and to the point. You may want to explain further in a conversation, but don't turn this into a venting situation and spend a lot of time and energy telling the client how difficult he is. At this point, you are no longer negotiating; you are moving on. Use classic lines: "This isn't working out" or "Another firm will be able to better serve your needs." Most difficult clients have heard it before. Stay firm and be professional in wrapping up the details of your work. Honor your confidentiality agreements, and return all of their materials as promptly as possible.

Measuring Results

Measuring the results of your public relations efforts is not easy, but it can be done. Some clients will want to measure your performance through sales leads generated and press clips. While these are easy to count, they are not always the best indicator of what you've done. The value of your services is better measured in what the market thinks of your clients, and that's more challenging to measure.

Your clients should want to evaluate the effectiveness, efficiency, and cost-effectiveness of their public relations efforts, and they may ask for your assistance in doing this. Ideally, you should begin any campaign with some specific and measurable goals, and those goals should be tied to the overall goals of the organization. Instead of measuring PR as a total entity, recommend that your clients measure individual PR activities, such as an individual program or particular special event.

There are three basic areas you'll want to measure: outputs, which are the specific tactics that you use; outtakes, which are the impact of those tactics on the attitude, beliefs, or awareness of the targeted public; and outcomes, which are the business results of the tactics. There is no single, all-encompassing research tool or technique that can be used to measure and evaluate PR effectiveness. You might analyze media content, evaluate search engine rankings, conduct polls and surveys, hold focus groups, or use other measuring methodologies.

Be careful when evaluating media content. While it's valuable, it's only part of the measurement process. You can count the number of times your client is mentioned in the media, but you don't know from that whether the target audiences saw the messages and, if they did, if they responded to them.

It's not a good idea to make a direct comparison between PR effectiveness and advertising. Your client has control over the content and placement of advertising, but not over what media outlets do with your PR efforts. Also, the fact that advertising and PR are perceived differently by the public needs to be considered.

The bottom line on measurement is that it's not "gee whiz" information, it's critical to demonstrate the impact of public relations on corporate objectives and on managing a company's reputation.

Interview Guide

Before the Interview

Before the interview is a good time to develop a rapport with the reporter and at the same time exert your rights as a spokesperson. Be assertive while maintaining a courteous and friendly demeanor. Reporters know that the better prepared you are, the better the interview will be. You don't need to ask all of these questions; choose the ones you feel will be most helpful. It's also a good idea to research the reporter ahead of time if you can. Just do an internet search on the reporter's name to see what type of work he does.

- What is the publication or broadcast outlet?
- What is the reporter's deadline? Most reporters work on tight deadlines. You need to know how much time is available so you can prepare and still give the reporter time to complete his research and finish the story.
- Who is the ultimate audience? To answer questions and provide information that will be appropriate, you need to know who the listeners, viewers, or readers will be.
- When will the results of the interview (article or broadcast) appear? Reporters usually do not provide you with copies of the published or broadcast interview but they will let you know when they expect it to appear so you can find it yourself.
- Who else is the reporter interviewing? This may reveal the angle of the piece and what types of questions (or accusations) you may have to answer.
- How will the interview be done and how will it be used? Is it a live broadcast? Taped? If taped, will it be edited? Will you be in a studio or by remote? By telephone? Face-to-face?
- When will the interview take place and how much time is necessary? If possible, choose a time when you are at your best. It's OK to set time limits; for most interviews, 20 to 30 minutes is sufficient. The reporter should be able to tell you how much time he needs.

During the Interview

- You have the right to record the interview and you may want to do so. If the subject matter is sensitive or complex, this will let you confirm that

Interview Guide, continued

your quotes are accurate. It's also a good way to hone your interviewing skills because you can review and critique what you said and how you said it later. If you choose to record the interview, let the journalist know what you're doing.

- Answer all of the reporter's questions. If you don't know the answer, be honest and say something like, "I'll have to get back to you on that." If the question is about something proprietary or confidential, indicate that you can't reveal that information.
- Know your message and deliver it often. This is your opportunity to share the information you want the world to know. Bridge from what you're asked to what you want to say.
- Stick to your area of expertise. Don't allow the reporter to pressure you into making comments you're not qualified to give.
- Don't let the reporter rush you to answer or cut you off. You are there to deliver your message and you have the right to be heard.
- Avoid being manipulated. Don't let the reporter put words in your mouth or define your vocabulary. Don't answer unrealistic hypothetical questions.
- Maintain your composure no matter how hard it might be.
- Maintain a proper facial expression. If it's appropriate, smile. If a serious, somber look is more suitable to the situation, adopt that expression.

General Do's and Don'ts

- Do remember that you are always "on the record." This includes during an interview as well as in casual conversations and other locations where you interact with reporters.
- Do speak in complete sentences, avoid giving one-word answers.
- Do be enthusiastic.
- Do correct factual inaccuracies in the questions you're asked.
- Do use anecdotes to illustrate your points.
- Do mention your organization, product, book, or whatever you're promoting as often as you can.

Interview Guide, continued

- Don't ask for a list of questions in advance. Some writers may offer them, and if they do, that's great. But most will simply tell you the general direction they expect the interview to take.
- Don't say "no comment." If you can't answer a question, say so and briefly explain why.
- Don't ask to have anything you said edited out before broadcast or publication.
- Don't use professional jargon or statistics your audience won't understand.
- Don't argue with a reporter.

Sample Media Policy

Effective and accurate communications with the media are important to our company and we make every effort to accommodate the media. Our goal is to balance the needs of reporters, our customers, our employees, and our company. Only individuals authorized to do so may speak on behalf of the company.

Inquiries from the media should be referred to [insert name, title, contact information] who will route the inquiry to the appropriate authorized spokesperson. Those who are authorized to respond to media inquiries should follow these guidelines:

- Find out who the reporter represents and be familiar with that publication or broadcast outlet.
- Treat all reporters, editors, producers, and other media representatives with courtesy and respect at all times.
- Media inquiries should be responded to promptly, if possible within one hour.
- Provide media representatives with appropriate background material, including media kits, either prior to or at the time of an interview.
- Be truthful and accurate. Don't exaggerate or speculate. Be as candid as possible without revealing confidential or proprietary information.
- Avoid commenting on other companies or people, particularly in a disparaging or defamatory way.
- Record or take notes on any media interview and forward that information to [insert name of designated individual] as soon as possible.
- Do not comment on pending litigation.

6

PR and the Internet

New technologies are creating significant implications for public relations and it is essential that public relations practitioners pay attention and educate their clients appropriately. The "rules" are changing as emerging technologies continue to transform the ways the public accesses information. "As audiences have increased their use of the internet and have grown more savvy with digital media of all types, public relations have needed to evolve with them," observes John V. Pavlik, Ph.D., in *Mapping the Consequences of Technology on Public Relations*, a report published by the Institute for Public Relations. "Audience members, or members of often key publics, maintain their own websites, blogs, or podcasts, often circumventing traditional media outlets. These citizen-produced online media can be influential and widely seen, and accounting for them may be essential to a public relations campaign."

The Internet's Impact on PR Strategies

The internet has become a daily tool for journalists and editors who use it for e-mail, to do research, and to find new sources and experts, press releases, and new angles on topics. Virtually all journalists go online for at least part of their story research.

Increasingly, journalists will check out corporate websites for information, which is why your clients need to have a clearly marked, easy-to-navigate press room on their sites that includes background information, a brief company history, news releases, bios and photos of key personnel, articles by other sources, and contact information. You will also need to incorporate online technologies such as blogs, podcasts, and videos into your clients' PR strategy.

Tip...

Smart Tip

Regardless of the medium, writing quality is still a deciding factor in effective communication. Be sure all your written materials are crisp, clear, accurate, and styled for your intended audience.

A Web Presence Is Essential

It is absolutely essential that your clients have a professional and functional web presence. This means a well-designed, eye-appealing, user-friendly website that will serve your clients' publics as well as being search-engine friendly. Unless your client is in the website design business or is large enough to have an IT and graphics-design department with these skills, it's almost always better for them to hire a professional designer than to do it themselves.

There are a number of fairly simple web design software packages on the market that are relatively inexpensive and easy to learn, making it tempting for many small-business owners to handle this process in-house. But that's not a great idea. The difference between a professionally designed site and one created by an amateur can range from subtle to obvious and can have a significant impact on a company's image and public relations.

"Getting a website online is not rocket science, but getting an *effective* website online is a lot more involved than it looks," says Elise Cronin-Hurley, owner of Liseydreams Web & Graphic Design in Winter Park, Florida. "Good design can elicit trust and interest in your client's commodity, but it is only one aspect of an effective site. A good web designer will seamlessly blend together design that communicates the company's vision with user-friendly navigation and search engine optimization to build a site that truly accomplishes what the client needs."

Some of your clients will have their own in-house team of IT and graphics people who can design and launch websites. Those who do should still consider using an outside consultant to evaluate the true usability of the site. Those who don't should outsource the job. "Poor design is at best a waste of time and money, and at worst detrimental to your company's image," Cronin-Hurley says. "I tell my clients that they are the experts in their fields and have valuable insight and input in the development of their site, but they need to focus on their core business, whatever that

Techno Tools

Public relations firms are using these online/social media tools to help guide clients through the changing communications landscape:

Tool	Percentage
Blogs	84%
Podcasts	60%
RSS	53%
Microsites	53%
Ineractive portals	42%
Mobile marketing	33%
Wikis	22%

Source: Council of Public Relations Firms

happens to be, and let me focus on the development of their websites, because that is *my* core business," Cronin-Hurley says.

The web is an incredibly dynamic tool. Recent trends in website development have more to do with function than design, so they are not always immediately visible. Suggest that your clients regularly evaluate the design, functionality, and search engine placement of their websites. "There was a time when websites were pretty much static and many became stale online brochures. The way we use the web has changed the demands of the web and websites. Today, some companies' websites function mainly to disseminate information, some are online stores, and others are portals to interconnectivity. No site should be static. The search engines can tell and so can the public at large. Does your website express that your company is dynamic, current, and exciting? If the site was designed even just a few years ago, it is probably now noticeably out of date," Cronin-Hurley says.

This doesn't mean you or your clients need a lot of bells and whistles purely for the sake of having them. For example, Cronin-Hurley says, "Motion and sound can be dramatic and effective, and pull people into your site, or they can be absolutely annoying, cause longer download times, and drive people away. Every element on your site should have a purpose that matches the overall purpose of your site."

As a public relations professional, you may want to align yourself with one or more topnotch website designers so that you have the resources to help your clients in this area when necessary.

Reaching the Public Through Blogs

They started as minor league sites on the internet and were known as web logs—a term that morphed into "blogs" as the sites exploded in popularity. What has become known as the blogosphere (a collective term encompassing all blogs and their interconnections) has become a powerful communications force and should be a key element in every company's public relations strategy. Bloggers can set trends, turn an obscure product into the next "big thing," destroy reputations and careers, expose wrongdoing, and turn ordinary people into instant celebrities.

Posting to a blog is as fast and simple as sending an e-mail. It is that speed and ease that make blogs a double-edged sword—it's all too easy to post something to a blog and regret it later. A number of sites make it simple to launch a blog in minutes for free or a nominal charge. Or you can purchase blogging software that lets you design, manage, and host blogs on your own servers.

Text Messaging Terminology

Here are a few examples of terms and characters used in text messages. It's a shorthand-type code that you should become familiar with.

ADIP	Another day in paradise
AND	Any day now
AFAICT	As far as I can tell
Affair	As far as I remember/recall
AWCIGO	And where can I get one
AYT	Are you there?
DGT	Don't go there
Treeware	Documentation
GWTL	Get with the lingo
HHIS	Hanging head in shame
Hhok	Ha ha only kidding
Mstke	Mistake
MWBRL	More will be revealed later
PTMM	Please tell me more
RBTL	Read between the lines
Xxxwrds	Rude words
FUD	Spreading fear uncertainty and disinformation
SHTSI	Somebody had to say it
W3s	Websites
Wdyt	What do you think
Y3	Yadda yadda yadda

Source: lingo2word.com

As a PR professional, you need to study blogs from the perspective of guiding your clients in getting them set up, what sort of content to post on them, and how to get the most benefit from them. In addition, you need to monitor the blogosphere for posts about your clients and subjects of interest to them. Part of your clients' blogging strategy should include linking to and posting comments on other blogs.

Podcasts, Twitter, Text Messages, Cell Phones, and More

Podcasts are digital files distributed over the internet for playback on portable media players and computers. Twitter is a website and service that lets users send short text messages from their cell phones to a group of friends or to blogs they can be valuable in a fast-breaking news situation.

The increased use of cell phones for text messages, e-mail, and internet access, and even online games should also be factored into your PR strategy. Sponsoring online games is an increasingly popular way to reach young publics. And social networking sites such as MySpace and Facebook have enormous implications for public relations.

> **Fun Fact**
>
> The first electronically transmitted press release was sent to 12 media outlets in New York by PR Newswire on March 8, 1954.

Keep in mind that by the time you read this, Twitter may have morphed into something else or have been replaced by a new technology. The online games that were popular last year may disappear by next year. And who knows what the next generation of cell phones will be able to do? As a public relations professional, you need to pay attention, monitor the trends and technologies, and adjust your strategic perspective accordingly.

Online Press Releases as a Marketing Tool

Press releases used to be sent exclusively to the media, generally by snail mail or fax, and the media functioned as gatekeepers, determining how much, if any, of your information the public ever saw. Today, savvy companies don't care if reporters even see some of their news releases, because those releases are targeted to search engines and the ultimate consumer.

Using press releases on the internet as a marketing tool is called marketing PR and it has become a very effective way to communicate with the public. Such press releases are generally keyword rich and include live links so the reader can go straight to your client's website for more information. These releases are not targeted to the media but rather to the ultimate consumer who uses the internet to gather information. They can be released through online wire services as well as posted on your client's site. They should be written in a style appropriate for the targeted reader and are typically longer and include more anecdotes and testimonials than a traditional press release does.

"News releases must also be adapted to cell phone and mobile media formats," advises Pavlik. "Embedding links within content is also important, enabling consumers to immediately act on content or messages of interest."

Video News Releases

Video news releases (VNRs) emerged in the 1980s as a video version of the traditional press release. Many were amateurish and most were clearly self-promotional. Tapes were mailed or sent by courier to television stations in the hopes that all or some of the VNR would make it on to the evening news. With technological advances, "the VNR has evolved into a sophisticated public relations tool and a frequent part of television news, particularly at the local level," notes Pavlik. "New technologies have made it increasingly effective to distribute VNRs in digital format via satellite or other broadband technologies. Typically, journalists can view or download VNRs before deciding whether to use them."

Beware!

Once something is posted on the internet, it is out there forever. Even though you may take the post down, chances are it's been archived by another site and will continue to be available to viewers.

Just as it's no longer essential to use traditional news channels for written press releases, VNRs are now available online on corporate websites and sites such as YouTube.

Free Article Sites

A great way to spread your clients' messages across the internet is through various free article sites. These sites have vast libraries of articles that are available for anyone who wants to download them for free and use them on their websites, blogs, in e-zines and other online publications, and elsewhere.

Most of these articles are short (about 400 to 600 words), keyword rich, and tightly focused. For public relations purposes, they may be written by an independent author who quotes your client, or by your client as part of your campaign to establish her as a recognized expert in a particular subject or industry.

Don't just recycle press releases and post them to the free article sites. The better sites will recognize what you've done and reject the pieces to protect their own reputations. Make the effort to create a well-written original piece that has value for the reader. It's OK to post the same article on multiple sites as long as the site doesn't have an exclusivity policy.

Search Engines

It's essential that you have a basic understanding of search engines and how they work so that you can guide your clients on issues such as search engine optimization and search engine marketing. A search engine is a type of software that searches the internet for information and returns sites that provide that information. There are two basic types: crawler-based search engines and human-powered directories that gather their information in different ways.

Crawler-based search engines "crawl" or "spider" through the web and create their listings automatically. Users search through what the software has found. A human-powered directory depends on submissions by people and a search looks only in the descriptions provided. In the web's early days, search engines were one or the other type; today, it's common for search engines to return results based on both crawler-based and human-powered listings.

Search engine optimization is the practice of designing web pages so that they will rank as high as possible in results from search engine sites. You can do this honestly by making the web page clearly describe its subject, making sure it contains truly useful information, including accurate information in Meta tags, and getting other sites to link to the page. Or you can do this dishonestly by attempting to deceive the search engine software with inaccurate Meta tags and other gimmicks. The dishonest route might occasionally work in the short-term, but it can get you blacklisted by the search engines. The long-term damage isn't worth it.

Search engine marketing involves search engine optimization but also includes other online website marketing strategies, including various types of advertising and other marketing programs offered by search engines. While search engine marketing is not a public relations function, you should be aware of what strategies your clients are using in this area so you can work in concert with them.

What's Not to Like?

The internet and all its capabilities has revolutionized how public relations practitioners function and generated a tremendous amount of opportunity for savvy users. It's fast, inexpensive—and absolutely essential for success in the future.

"As communication technology has evolved, U.S. society has come to expect ever more rapid communications," notes Pavlik. "This can be both a boon and a bane to human existence. For public relations, it often means great expectations for fast and efficient communications between and among organizations and their publics."

7

Building Media Relationships

Media relationships are a critical element of successful public relations, and there are no shortcuts to building them. Cultivating media contacts is an ongoing process for successful PR professionals.

First Step: Identify

The first step in building media relationships is to identify the media members who work in areas that are important to you and your clients. You can buy media lists and directories, but you need to refine the information they contain to suit your own purposes.

A way to build a more effective list is to read the publications you want to see your clients in, identify the writers who cover the appropriate topics, and initiate a contact. In most cases this can be done by e-mail. Simply send a message that you saw the writer's byline in whatever publication, you represent clients that may be appropriate sources in the future, but you want to make sure you send the writer information he can use. Ask if the writer will answer a few questions by e-mail or if she would prefer that you call. In this initial contact, your goal is to get only basic information including contact preferences and topics covered.

Most print and online publications include contact information for the author at the end of the article, either an e-mail address or a website in print publications, or a link in online publications. You can usually tell by a quick check of the masthead information whether a writer is staff or freelance—staff writers are usually identified as such and freelancers are generally listed in the "contributing" category. Remember that publications often have different teams of writers working on their print and online editions, so don't assume one contact at any given media outlet is sufficient.

For broadcast outlets, check the show credits for the producers' names. Contact information for local media outlets is usually easy to get with just a quick phone call to the station or a look at its website. National media is a little more challenging, but with perseverance, you can find out who you need to contact. You can also search in online directories for television and radio show producers.

Remember that online publication opportunities include more than just the digital version of print products. Bloggers have become very powerful in the media world; read blogs and get bloggers on your media list. Look beyond standard broadcast outlets as well. Podcasts allow anyone with the initiative to do so to launch an online radio show, and those programs are always on the lookout for hot topics and interesting guests.

Bright Idea

Make friends in the media before you need them. Establish relationships so that when something happens, reporters know who you are. And don't overlook young journalists at small outlets—the ones that are talented and driven will be moving up, and you want to be on their contact list when they do.

Information to Keep on File about Media Representatives

Note: Set up your own database in whatever system works for you

Name: ______________________________

Company/Publication(s): ______________________________

Staff or freelance: ______________________________

Address: ______________________________

Website: ______________________________

Telephone numbers (office, home, cell, fax): ______________________________

____

E-mail: ______________________________

Alternative e-mail: ______________________________

Preferred contact method (1st, 2nd, 3rd): ______________________________

Type of media: ______________________________

Categories/subjects: ______________________________

Personal information (marital status, children, hobbies, birthday) ____________

____

Results (notes of when the media rep has acted on information you supplied)

____

____

Contact history: ______________________________

Comments (general notes about the media rep that don't fit any other category)

____

____

____

Date of last update: ______________________________

Build the Relationship

Set up a database with details about all your media contacts. Use whatever contact management system works for you; what's important is that the information be easy to use. The list on page 59 is a good guide for the type of information you need to keep on file.

Pay attention to what media contacts tell you about the type of stories they do and the way they want to work with PR professionals. Most journalists recognize the value that a good PR contact brings to the process of researching stories and finding good sources, but they have little patience with or use for PR reps who don't demonstrate a solid understanding of their needs.

To get an idea of what annoys journalists, take a look at www.angryjournalist.com, a blog set up for "the underpaid, overworked, frustrated, pissed off, and ignored media professionals to publicly and anonymously vent their anger." Here's one post on that site every PR practitioner should take to heart: "Stupid, stupid, stupid public relations practitioners who send me things that clearly demonstrate that they have no clue what I do, that they NEVER read my publication, and they have no clue what their clients do. And then they quietly wonder why they never get into my stories?!?!?!?!"

PR is *Not* Telemarketing

"Dialing for dollars" doesn't work in PR. Big PR firms often put their junior people on the phone calling journalists and reading scripts pitching a particular client or product. Not only does that not work, it's annoying to busy journalists and editors.

One freelance journalist tells this story: "I received a phone call from a big New York-based PR firm. The rep raced through a script about something I couldn't use, and when he finished, I politely told him his client didn't fit anything I was working on at the moment. I added that what I needed was ideas and resources on business insurance. He began telling me about another company—one that refills toner cartridges. When I asked what that had to do with insurance, he said, 'Nothing.' I have talked with telemarketers who listened better than this guy."

If you're going to call a media representative, personalize it and make it about something that the rep can use. And always begin the conversation by asking if it's a convenient time to talk.

Beware!

Never call a media representative and suggest that he write a profile on your client; that's one of the quickest ways to get on a journalist's "ignore" list. Only offer legitimate story ideas and indicate that your client would make a good resource for the piece.

When you contact a media representative, remember that it's always about him, never about you or your client. Your client may be paying the bill, but when you're talking to a reporter, your job is to help her get a good story.

Once you have relationships established with journalists, they will often call you when they're looking for a source. If you have a client that's a good fit, great. If you don't, be honest. And if you can refer a reporter to someone who is not your client but would make a good source, do it. Reporters appreciate and respect that level of professionalism, and it will keep them coming back to you for sources in the future.

Keep your media list up-to-date. Once a year, go through the list to make sure you have the right contact information and other details. Journalists are mobile, and even if they stay with the same publication, they may change beats. Once you've established a contact, maintain it.

Don't Spam

E-mail is a preferred contact method for many journalists and most make an e-mail address available to the public. They welcome good story pitches and useful information, but they hate spam as much as anyone else. Get permission before you add a media representative to your press release distribution list. And even when you have permission to send e-mails, don't send every single release to every single person on your list. Be selective and target your releases.

Online thought leadership and viral marketing strategist David Meerman Scott wrote this on his blog, WebInkNow.com:

> At every one of my speeches, I say PR people are spammers. That gets everyone's attention so I have an opportunity to explain what I mean.
>
> I get several hundred unsolicited press releases and PR pitches every week. Well over 99 percent of them are not targeted to me, instead they are sent to me because I am on various PR people's lists because of this blog, because of my books, and because I am a contributing editor to *EContent Magazine* and have written for a bunch of other publications. I'm getting the identical piece of spam e-mail as hundreds of other poor journalists.

To paraphrase the Wikipedia entry, spam is sending e-mail that is both unsolicited by the recipient and sent in substantively identical form to many recipients.

Chris Anderson, editor-in-chief of *Wired Magazine* and author of *The Long Tail* recently lamented that he gets 300 e-mails a day and he's had it. So he's blocked PR people and has published a list of those blocked on his blog.

Chris says: "So, fair warning: I only want two kinds of e-mail—those from people I know, and those from people who have taken the time to find out what I'm interested in and composed a note meant to appeal to that (I love those e-mails; indeed, that's why my e-mail address is public)."

I couldn't agree more.

At my speaking gigs, after I get people's attention by saying PR people are spammers and describe the worst practices, I also offer ideas on how to be successful with the media:

- Read our blogs.
- Comment on our blogs.
- Read our books.
- Read our publications (or watch and listen to our TV and radio shows).
- Attend our speaking gigs.
- Publish your own blog.
- Send well-crafted, personal e-mail telling us something that is interesting and helpful.

Fun Fact

Yellow journalism doesn't refer to a color, but rather is a pejorative reference to unethical and unprofessional practices by news organizations and journalists that feature scandal-mongering, sensationalism, and biased opinion masquerading as fact. The term was coined in the late nineteenth century when the practice was blatant and widespread. Though obvious yellow journalism disappeared for the most part in the early 1900s, it's still a good idea for readers to remain skeptical of news sources.

Journalism Comes in a Variety of Flavors

Journalism is defined as the "collection, preparation, and distribution of news and related commentary and feature materials through media such as pamphlets, newsletters, newspapers, magazines, radio, film, television, and books" [*Britannica Precise Encyclopedia*]. Within that definition are a number of journalism genres that are useful to understand when building media relationships and developing public relations strategies.

- *Advocacy journalism* intentionally and transparently adopts a nonobjective viewpoint, usually for some social or political purpose. It is intended to be factual and is usually produced by private media outlets, as opposed to governments.
- *Citizen journalism* is also known as public or participatory journalism. It is the process of citizens being actually involved in collecting, reporting, analyzing, and disseminating news and information.
- *Civic journalism* is as much an ideology as a practice, and treats readers and community members as participants rather than spectators in political and social processes.
- *Community journalism* is locally oriented coverage that typically focuses on city neighborhoods or individual suburbs rather than metropolitan, state, national, or world news. Media outlets such as community newspapers typically cover subjects larger news media do not, such as local school news and events (student achievements, sports, etc.), local crimes, zoning issues, and local issues that would usually not attract a broader interest.
- *Gonzo journalism* tends to blend fact and fiction to emphasize an underlying message. The writing is subjective, and the reporter is often a part of the story.
- *Investigative journalism* is when reporters deeply investigate an incident or issue, often involving a crime, corruption, or scandal. Investigative reports may take months or even years to complete.
- *Literary journalism*, also known as creative nonfiction and narrative journalism, uses literary styles and techniques to tell a factually accurate story.
- *New journalism* is a style popularized in the 1960s and 1970s that used literary techniques deemed unconventional at the time. Articles written in this style tend to be found in magazines rather than newspapers.
- *Opinion journalism* makes no claim of objectivity and features a subjective viewpoint usually with some social or political purpose, such as in newspaper columns, editorials, and editorial cartoons.
- *Visual journalism* combines words and images to convey information.
- *Watchdog journalism* seeks to hold accountable various public personalities and institutions whose functions impact social and political life.

  Source: Wikipedia

8

Grow Your Firm Through Professional Alliances

You may have decided to start your own firm because you want to be in business *for* yourself, but you can't succeed *by* yourself. Certainly you need clients, but you also need a network of resources. Especially when you're small, but no matter what size you eventually reach, you need professional alliances.

Other PR Agencies

Of course other agencies are your competition, but there will be times when they are much-needed allies. You may have an opportunity to partner with another agency to accomplish something for a client that you can't do alone. For example, let's say your client wants to hold a special event and you don't have the resources or expertise to coordinate the event itself. If you have a relationship with an agency that does that sort of work, you can team up to benefit each other while making the client happy.

Beware!

Before you enter into a joint project with another agency or hire a freelancer for a project, put all the details in writing, including appropriate noncompete and nondisclosure agreements.

Networking with other agency owners and staffers can be an invaluable source of information in the form of referrals and education. If you run across a prospective client that you can't handle—either because it doesn't fit your firm's niche or for any other reason—pass the referral along. Most professionals appreciate and reciprocate when they receive a lead. Other agencies can also be a resource for recommendations on freelancers and service providers.

Freelancers

Even big agencies with large staffs turn to freelancers on occasion. For smaller agencies, freelancers are essential for getting the client's work done.

Identify freelancers before you need them. Find out what they do, their areas of expertise, what they charge, and how quickly they typically turn work around. Build a database so you have that information readily available when it's needed. It's a good idea to have more than one resource for each skill in case your first choice isn't available when you call.

The typical freelancers you'll need include:

- *Writers.* Depending on your client base, you'll need people who can write press releases (both targeted to the media as well as marketing releases targeted to consumers); company materials such as press kit content; essays and articles; technical materials; scripts; speeches; and perhaps even marketing copy.
- *Photographers.* At the least, your clients should have professional headshots for inclusion in their media kits and on their websites—and no, snapshots won't work. The goal is attractive photographs, not mugshots. You may also

What Goes Around Comes Around

The principles of karma are alive and well in the business world. As you build your professional alliances, be willing to share information (as long as it is not proprietary or confidential) and help others even when there is no immediate benefit for you.

The freelancers and service providers you work with have the potential to be a great source of leads for you, so if you can help them find business from sources other than your company, it's a good investment. If you know of a company that is not a client but would be a good source for a media contact, pass the information along. People remember when you help them. It will come back to benefit you.

need photographers to help with a variety of other promotional photo needs.

- *Graphic artists/designers.* Typically the visually creative work will be left to the advertising department or agency, but you may occasionally need this type of work for one of your clients.
- *Website designers.* If your clients' online presence isn't up to par, you may need to provide the expertise to correct it.
- *Audio and video technicians.* You need access to people who can create and edit audio and video recordings for use as video news releases, podcasts, online videos, and so on.
- *Proofreaders and copyeditors.* It's a good idea to send critical writing projects to a proofreader and/or copyeditor prior to releasing those materials to the public.

Tip...

Smart Tip

Pay your freelancers promptly. Some agencies have a "we'll pay you when we get paid" policy, but that's not fair to the freelancer—who is working for *you*, not your client. Set reasonable payment terms with freelancers and stick to them.

Product and Service Providers

As with freelancers, you need a stable of reliable product and service providers both for your own needs and for the needs of your clients. Those resources include:

- *Printers.* Find printers who can handle standard business needs such as stationery and business cards, as well as printers who can do a great job on brochures, books, packaging, and more.
- *Promotional item vendors.* You need resources for customized items ranging from traditional mugs and T-shirts to more creative and unusual things. In addition to being a source for the actual item, these companies can also provide you with ideas for various promotional campaigns.
- *Web hosting.* You need an excellent web hosting service for your own firm as well as to refer your clients to if necessary.
- *Press release distribution.* Even though you will build your own targeted media lists, you should be familiar with the services of several online press release distribution services.

9

Structuring Your Business

Whether your goal is a solo homebased operation, a small family business, or a public relations empire, you need to start with a written business plan. This helps you think through what you're doing, see your strengths and weaknesses, and figure out ways to overcome challenges on paper before you have to face them in real life. Writing a business plan is not just a necessary chore; it creates the foundation and sets the vision for your company. If you're excited about your business, you'll enjoy the process of creating a plan for it.

Your business plan should include worst-case scenarios. You'll benefit from thinking ahead about what you'll do if things don't go as you want them to. Give consideration to things such as unreasonable clients, equipment breakdowns, employees who don't show up (even for valid reasons), uncollectible invoices, and other challenges that are part of doing business today.

As you put together your plan, keep in mind the business structure issues addressed in this chapter.

Naming Your Company

Your company name is an important marketing tool. A well-chosen name works very hard for you; choosing an ineffective name means you have to work much harder at marketing your public relations firm and letting people know what you have to offer.

Your company name should clearly identify what you do in a way that appeals to your target market. It should be short, catchy, and memorable. It should also be easy to pronounce and spell—people who can't say your company name may use you, but they won't refer anyone else to you. Many public relations firms include the names or initials of the principals in their name, along with what they do, such as Perkett PR, Inc., founded by Christine Perkett in Marshfield, Massachusetts. Others get more creative, such as Jason Mandell, Jason Thockmorton, and Jesse Odell, who formed LaunchSquad in San Francisco to provide PR to growing technology companies. There is no right or wrong way; choose something that works for you.

Once you've decided on two or three possibilities for your firm's name, take the following steps:

1. *Check the name for effectiveness and functionality*. Does it quickly and easily convey what you do? Is it easy to say and spell? Is it memorable in a positive way? Ask several of your friends and associates to serve as a focus group to help you evaluate the name's impact.
2. *Search for potential conflicts in your local market.* Find out if any other local or regional business serving your market area has a similar name that might confuse the public.
3. *Check for legal availability.* Exactly how you do this depends on the legal structure you choose. Typically, sole proprietorships and partnerships operating

under a name other than that of the owner(s) are required by the county, city, or state to register their fictitious name. Even if it's not required, it's a good idea because it means no one else can use that name. Sometimes it's as simple as filing for a DBA (doing business as). Corporations usually operate under their corporate name. In either case, you need to check with the appropriate regulatory agency to be sure the name you choose is available.

4. *Check for use on the Internet.* If someone else is already using your name as an address on the web, consider coming up with something else.
5. *Check to see if the name conflicts with any name listed on your state's trademark register.* Your state department of commerce can help you or direct you to the correct agency. You should also check with the trademark register maintained by the U.S. Patent and Trademark Office (PTO).

Once the name you've chosen passes these tests, you need to protect it by registering it with the appropriate state agency; again, your state department of commerce can help you. If you expect to be doing business on a national level, you should also register the name with the PTO.

Bright Idea

When naming your company, consider creating a word that doesn't exist. That's what companies like Exxon and Kodak did. Just be sure the syllables blend to make an ear-appealing sound and that the name is simple enough for people to remember. Also, make sure you haven't inadvertently come up with a name that means something negative in another language.

Choosing a Legal Structure

One of the first decisions you'll need to make about your PR firm is the legal structure of your company. This is an important decision. It affects your financial liability, the amount of taxes you pay, and the degree of ultimate control you have over the company. It also affects your ability to attract investors and ultimately sell the business. However, legal structure shouldn't be confused with operating structure. Your legal structure is the ownership structure, and the operating structure defines who makes management decisions and runs the company.

A sole proprietorship is owned by the proprietor; a partnership is owned by the partners; and a corporation is owned by the shareholders. Another business structure, the limited liability company (LLC), combines the tax advantages of a sole proprietorship with the liability protection of a corporation. The rules on LLCs vary by state; check with your state's department of corporations for the latest requirements.

Sole proprietorships and partnerships can be operated however the owners choose. In a corporation, the shareholders typically elect directors who, in turn, elect officers who then employ other people to run and work in the company. But it's entirely possible for a corporation to have only one shareholder and to essentially function as a sole proprietorship. In any case, how you plan to operate the company should not be a major factor in your choice of legal structures.

So what goes into choosing a legal structure? The first point is who is actually making the decision on the legal structure. If you're starting the company by yourself, you don't need to take anyone else's preferences into consideration. If there are multiple people involved, you need to consider how you're going to relate to each other in the business. You also need to consider the issue of asset protection and limiting your liability in the event things don't go as you expect.

Something else to think about is your target clients and what their perception will be of your structure. There is a tendency to believe that the legal form of a business has some relationship to the sophistication of the owners, with the sole proprietor as the least and the corporation as the most sophisticated. It will probably enhance your image if you form an LLC or incorporate.

Your image notwithstanding, the biggest advantage of forming a corporation is in the area of asset protection and making sure that the assets you don't want to put into the business don't stand liable for business debt. However, to take advantage of the protection a corporation offers, you must respect the corporation's identity. That means maintaining the corporation as a separate entity; keeping your corporate and personal funds separate, even if you are the sole shareholder; and following your state's rules regarding holding annual meetings and other record-keeping requirements.

You don't need an attorney to set up a corporation, LLC, or partnership. There are plenty of good do-it-yourself books and kits on the market, and most of the state agencies that oversee corporations have guidelines you can use. Even so, it's always a good idea to have a lawyer at least look over your documents before you file them, just to make sure they are complete and will allow you to truly function as you want.

Finally, remember that your choice of legal structure is not an irrevocable decision, although if you're going to make a switch, it's easier to go from the simpler forms to the more

Bright Idea

Sit down with your insurance agent every year and review your insurance needs, which are sure to change as your company grows. Also, insurance companies are always developing new products to meet the needs of the growing small-business market, and it's possible one of these new policies will be more appropriate for you.

sophisticated ones than vice versa. The typical pattern is to start as a sole proprietor and then move up to a corporation as the business grows. But if you need the asset protection of a corporation from the beginning, start out that way.

Insurance

It takes a lot to start a business, even a small one, so protect your investment with adequate insurance. If you're homebased, do not assume your homeowner's or renter's policy covers your business equipment; chances are, it doesn't. If you're located in a commercial facility, be prepared for your landlord to require proof of certain levels of liability insurance when you sign the lease. In either case, you need coverage for your equipment and supplies, and workers' compensation if you have employees.

Bright Idea

Be sure your insurance covers your clients' property while in your possession. This could include documents, product samples provided either for you or to be distributed to the media for review, promotional items, and anything else that you may have in your custody that you don't own.

A smart approach to insurance is to find an agent who works with professional service providers such as public relations and advertising firms. The agent should be willing to help you analyze your needs, evaluate what risks you're willing to accept and what risks you need to insure against, and work with you to keep your insurance costs down.

Typically, homebased PR firms want to make sure their equipment and supplies are covered against theft and damage by an act of God, such as fire or flood, and that they have some liability protection if someone (a client, supplier, or employee) is injured on their property. In most cases, one of the new insurance products designed for homebased businesses will provide sufficient coverage. Also, you will probably use your vehicle for business purposes, so make sure it is adequately covered.

If you opt for a commercial location, you'll need to meet the landlord's requirements for general liability coverage. You'll also want to cover your supplies, equipment, and fixtures. Once your business is up and running, consider

Smart Tip

Tip...

When you purchase insurance on your equipment and fixtures, ask what documentation the insurance company requires before you have to file a claim. That way, you'll be sure to maintain appropriate records, and the claims process will be easier.

When "I'm Sorry" Isn't Enough

Often, business mistakes can be handled with a sincere "I'm sorry" and perhaps an adjustment on the invoice. But what if your mistake, or maybe something you said or forgot to say, causes your client serious economic loss? To protect yourself from the cost of litigation and damages, you need errors and omissions (E&O) coverage.

E&O—also called professional liability insurance—covers professionals for unintentional errors or omissions they make in the rendering of their professional services. It pays both defense costs and damage awards.

Don't confuse E&O with general liability; it's not the same thing. E&O coverage is typically provided through a stand-alone policy, and is tailored to your particular service and risk factors. Your insurance agent can help you analyze your potential liabilities and determine how much coverage you need. And remember, whether you actually make a mistake or not, you can still be sued. In today's litigious business environment, E&O coverage is a good idea for all professional service providers.

business interruption insurance to replace lost revenue and cover related costs if you are ever unable to operate due to covered circumstances.

Licenses and Permits

Most cities and counties require business operators to obtain various licenses and permits to comply with local regulations. While you are still in the planning stages, check with your local planning and zoning department or city/county business license department to find out what licenses and permits you will need and how to obtain them. You may need some or all of the following:

Beware!

Be sure you keep all your licenses and permits current and pay any local or state fees on time. Very often, the penalties for late payments are far more costly than the initial license, permit, or fee.

- *Occupational license or permit.* This is typically required by the city (or county if you are not within an incorporated city) for just about every business operating within its jurisdiction. License fees are essentially a tax, and the rates vary widely based on the location and type of business. As part of the application process, the licensing bureau will check to make sure there are no zoning restrictions prohibiting you from operating.

> **Beware!**
> Find out what type of licenses and permits are required for your business while you're still in the planning stage. You may find out that you can't legally operate the business you're envisioning in the location of your choice, so give yourself time to make adjustments to your strategy before you've spent a lot of time and money trying to move in an impossible direction.

- *Fire department permit.* If your office is in a commercial location and/or open to the public, you may be required to have a permit from the local fire department.
- *Sign permit.* Many cities and suburbs have sign ordinances that restrict the size, location, and sometimes the lighting and type of sign you can use in front of your business. Landlords may also impose their own restrictions. Most residential areas forbid signs altogether. To avoid costly mistakes, check regulations and secure the written approval of your landlord before you invest in a sign.

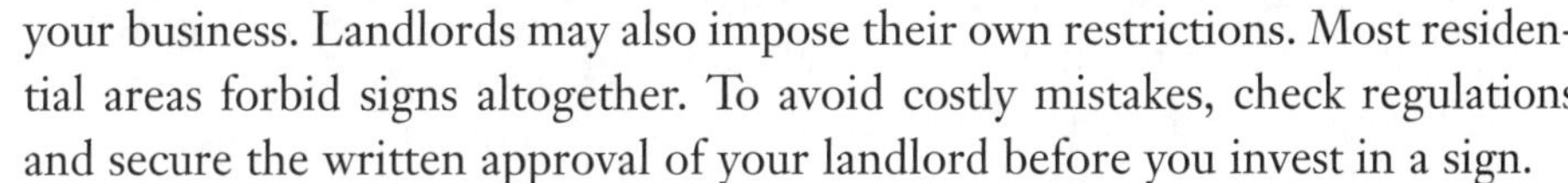

- *State licenses.* Many states require people engaged in certain occupations to hold licenses or occupational permits. Often, these people must pass state examinations before they can conduct business. States commonly require licensing for auto mechanics, plumbers, electricians, building contractors, collection agents, insurance agents, real estate brokers, repossessors, and personal service providers such as doctors, nurses, barbers, cosmetologists, etc. It is highly unlikely that you will need a state license to operate your public relations business, but it's a good idea to check with your state's occupation licensing entity to be sure.

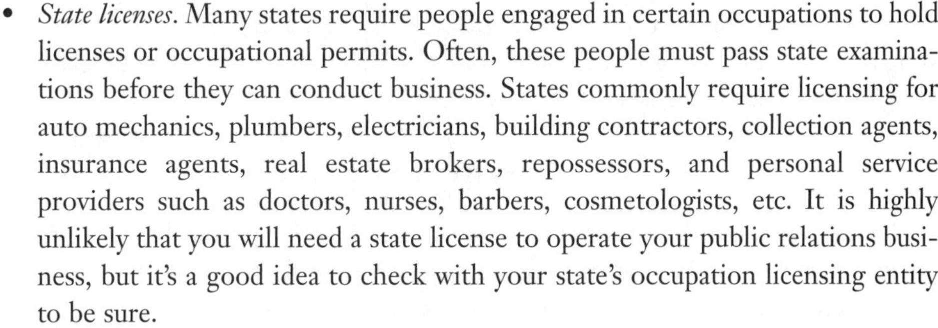

Professional Advisors

As a business owner, you may be the boss, but you can't be expected to know everything. You will occasionally need to turn to professionals for information and assistance. It's a good idea to establish a relationship with these professionals before you get into a crisis situation.

To shop for a professional service provider, ask friends and associates for recommendations. You might also check with your local chamber of commerce or trade association for referrals. Find someone who understands the public relations industry and appears eager to work with you. Contact the Better Business Bureau and the appropriate state licensing agency before committing yourself.

The professional service providers you are likely to need include the following:

Attorney

You need a lawyer who understands and practices in the area of business and contracts, who is honest, and who appreciates your patronage. In most parts of the United States, there are many lawyers willing to compete fiercely for the privilege of serving you. Interview several and choose one with whom you feel comfortable. Be sure to clarify the fee schedule ahead of time, and get your agreement in writing. Keep in mind that good commercial lawyers don't come cheap; if you want good advice, you must be willing to pay for it. Your attorney should review all contracts, leases, letters of intent, and other legal documents before you sign them. They can also help you with collecting bad debts and establishing personnel policies and procedures. Of course, if you are unsure of the legal ramifications of any situation, call your attorney immediately.

Tip...

Smart Tip

Not all attorneys are created equal, and you may need more than one. For example, the lawyer who can best guide you in contract negotiations may not be the most effective counsel when it comes to employment issues. Ask about areas of expertise and specialization before retaining a lawyer.

Accountant

Among your outside advisors, your accountant is likely to have the greatest impact on the success or failure of your business. If you are forming a corporation, your accountant should counsel you on tax issues during start-up. On an ongoing basis, your accountant can help you organize the statistical data concerning your business, assist in charting future actions based on past performance, and advise you on your overall financial strategy regarding purchasing, capital investment, and other matters related to your business goals. A good accountant also serves as a tax advisor, making sure you are in compliance with all applicable regulations but also that you don't overpay any taxes.

Insurance Agent

A good independent insurance agent can assist you with all aspects of your business insurance from general liability to employee benefits and probably even handle your personal lines as well. Look for an agent who works with a wide range of insurers and understands your particular business. This agent should be willing to explain the details of various types of coverage, to consult with you to determine the most appropriate coverage, to help you understand the degree of risk you are taking, to work with you to develop risk-reduction programs, and to assist in expediting any claims.

Banker

You need a business bank account and a relationship with a banker. Don't just choose the bank you've always used for your personal banking; it may not be the best bank for your business. Interview several bankers before making a decision. Remember, you're the customer. Banks are *not* doing you a favor by allowing you to put your money in their institution, you're doing them a favor by allowing them to serve you. Once your account is open, maintain a relationship with the banker. Periodically sit down and review your accounts and the services you use to make sure you have the most appropriate package for your situation.

Consultants

The consulting industry is booming—and for good reason. Consultants can provide valuable, objective input on all aspects of your business. (Keep in mind that as a public relations professional, you will often wear a consultant's hat as you work with your clients.) Consider hiring a business consultant to evaluate your business plan or a marketing consultant to assist you in that area. When you're ready to hire employees, a human resources consultant may help you avoid some costly mistakes. If you're starting your business with family members, it might help to consult with an expert in the areas of both family dynamics in business and succession planning. Consulting fees vary widely depending on the individual's experience, location, and field of expertise. If you can't afford to hire a consultant, consider contacting the business school at the nearest college or university and hiring an MBA student to help you.

Bright Idea

Prepare for the future. Certainly it's understandable that at this point your primary focus is on getting started, but you also need to think about the future. Develop a succession plan that is reviewed and revised annually. Know how leadership will be transferred when it becomes necessary—either through voluntary or involuntary departures.

Sales Tax

Laws regarding the collection and remittance of sales tax vary by state, so you need to check with your state's department of revenue to see what you're required to do. Many states treat products and services differently when it comes to sales tax; for example, you may not be required to charge tax on fees for your services, but you may have to collect sales tax on any tangible items you provide your clients. Generally when you buy things to resell, you don't have to pay sales tax on the purchase but you must collect it on the sale.

Typically, you'll be required to file your state sales tax return quarterly, but this varies by state and can often be negotiated based on your volume. If you are in a state that does not tax services and your taxable sales are likely to be limited to a very small amount or infrequent transactions, such as making the occasional printing or premium item purchase for your clients, you may even be allowed to file annually.

Whatever you do, don't be careless about sales tax. Failing to properly collect and remit sales tax is a serious crime with very unpleasant consequences.

Computer Expert

Your computer is your most valuable physical asset, so if you don't know much about computers, find someone to help you select a system and the appropriate software, someone who will be available to help you maintain, troubleshoot, and expand your system as you need it.

Create Your Own Advisory Board

Not even the President of the United States is expected to know everything. That's why he surrounds himself with advisors, experts in particular areas who provide knowledge and information to help him make decisions. Savvy small-business owners use a similar strategy.

You can assemble a team of volunteer advisors to meet with you periodically to offer advice and direction. Because this isn't an official or legal entity, you have a great deal of latitude in how you set it up. Advisory boards can be structured to help with the direct operation of your company and to keep you informed on various business, legal, and financial trends that may affect you. Use these tips to set up your advisory board:

- *Structure a board that meets your needs.* Generally, you'll want a legal advisor, an accountant, a marketing expert, a human resources person, and perhaps a financial advisor. You may also want successful entrepreneurs from other industries who understand the basics of business and will view your operation with a fresh eye.

When It's Time to Go

Getting practical industry experience before you start your own business by working for another public relations firm or in a corporate PR department is a great idea. But when do you tell your boss about your plans to start your own business?

There's no one-size-fits-all answer. You need to determine where you stand ethically, legally, and practically. Take any employment-related contracts you have signed—including noncompete and confidentiality agreements—along with your employee handbook to an attorney. This is especially important if your new firm will either compete with or use information (such as media contacts) you obtained from your current employer. A lawyer can review those documents, let you know whether or not you are violating the agreements, and help you understand what potential litigation you may face.

Keep in mind that you *can* be fired for starting your own business. Most states are at-will employment states, which means you can be terminated for any reason or no reason, as long as there is no discrimination involved. So be prepared to be shown the door as soon as your plans become known.

What about trying to start something on the side and building it as long as you can while still working full time? The risk you're taking there is the image you're projecting to your clients. If you're sneaking around behind your employer's back and violating your employment contract, you're sending a message of questionable judgment and ethics to your clients and associates. Also, the nature of the PR industry puts practitioners in a visible position. It's best to make a clean break when you're ready to go.

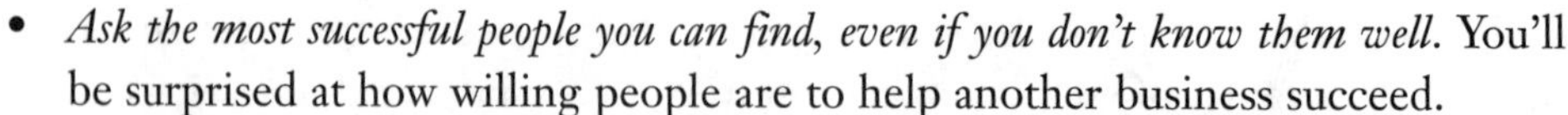

- *Ask the most successful people you can find, even if you don't know them well.* You'll be surprised at how willing people are to help another business succeed.
- *Be clear about what you are trying to do.* Let your prospective advisors know what your goals are and that you don't expect them to take on an active management role or to assume any liability for your company or for the advice they offer.
- *Don't worry about compensation.* Advisory board members are rarely compensated with more than lunch or dinner. Of course, if a member of your board provides a direct service, for example, an attorney reviews a contract or an accountant prepares a financial statement, then they should be paid at their normal rate. But that's not part of their job as an advisory board member. Keep in mind that, even though you don't write them a check, your advisory board members will likely benefit in a variety of tangible and intangible ways. Being on your board will expose them to ideas and perspectives they may not otherwise see and will also expand their own network.
- *Consider the group dynamics when holding meetings.* You may want to meet with all the members together or in small groups of one or two. It all depends on how they relate to each other and what you need to accomplish.
- *Ask for honesty, and don't be offended when you get it.* Your pride might be hurt when someone points out something you're doing wrong, but the awareness will be beneficial in the long run.
- *Learn from failure as well as success.* Encourage board members to tell you about their mistakes so you can avoid making them.
- *Respect the contribution your board members are making.* Let them know you appreciate how busy they are, and don't abuse or waste their time.
- *Make it fun.* You are, after all, asking these people to donate their time, so create a pleasant atmosphere.
- *Listen to every piece of advice.* Stop talking and listen. You don't have to follow every piece of advice, but you need to hear it.
- *Provide feedback to the board.* Good or bad, let the board members know what you did and what the results were.

10

Locating and Equipping Your Business

One of the appealing aspects of a public relations firm is that your physical startup requirements are relatively small. When it comes to the actual site of your business, you have two choices: homebased or a commercial location. You can be extremely successful in either venue; your decision will depend on your individual resources and goals.

In any business, but especially this one, a professional image is a critical element of success. Homebased operations are very accepted in today's business world (in fact, many customers prefer dealing with homebased suppliers because they have lower overhead and can therefore charge less), but you still need to present the appearance of being a serious business, even though you may choose to work from your house. And if you opt for a commercial location, it should be one that is compatible with your goals and image.

Be sure you have plenty of storage room for client files and supplies. You may keep product samples around or if you promote authors, you'll likely have a supply of their books on hand. In fact, your clients' "stuff" could take up more room than your own equipment and supplies. By the way, if you are keeping items on hand that belong to your clients, your contract should address that in terms of responsibility, making judgments about whom to give things to, insurance, and returning those items if your relationship ends.

Homebased Operations

Many PR firms start from home with the goal of moving into commercial space as soon as they are established with a few clients, and this is an excellent strategy. The major benefit of starting a homebased business is the fact that it significantly reduces the amount of startup and initial operating capital you'll need. But there's more to consider than simply the upfront cash. You need to be conveniently located so you can get to your clients' offices without wasting a lot of time in your car.

Next, think about your home itself. Do you have a separate room for an office, or will you have to work at the dining room table? Can you set up a comfortable workstation with all the tools and equipment you'll need? Can you separate your work area from the rest of the house so you can have privacy when you're working and get away from "the office" when you're not?

Tip...

Smart Tip

Whether you are homebased or commercial-based, be sure your office has adequate electrical capacity. You'll need an ample supply of "clean" current without fluctuations that could damage your equipment. You'll also need plenty of outlets so you can safely plug in all your equipment. Many older office buildings and homes are lacking in this area. Consult with an electrician or a representative from your local power company to make sure your office has the capacity to support your needs.

Commercial Locations

If you decide on a commercial location, your range of options is fairly broad, and your choice should be guided largely by the specific services you want to provide and the market you want to reach. Starting in a commercial location requires more initial cash than starting from home, but you'll have a degree of credibility that is hard to earn in a homebased office. You'll also have space to store the equipment and supplies you'll use in the course of your business, and create a setup that is more efficient and practical than what you might be able to do in a spare bedroom. You'll probably only need 200 to 400 square feet at first, and you should be able to find an office that size in a good location at a fairly reasonable price.

Choosing the Right Equipment

Having the right equipment is a critical part of being able to provide the services your clients want and need. On the plus side, compared with many other types of businesses, your equipment needs are minimal. However, choosing the right pieces for your particular operation will take some research. Here's a quick rundown of the basic equipment you'll most likely need.

> **Bright Idea**
>
> Consider investing in a natural or ergonomic keyboard rather than the standard flat design. The ergonomic design is slightly curved and fits the natural positioning of the hands, which reduces hand and wrist stress and the risk of repetitive motion problems such as carpal tunnel syndrome.

Computers and Related Equipment

- *Computer*. You don't necessarily need the "latest and greatest" in computer power, but you need a reasonably up-to-date system that will allow you to handle large digital files, burn CDs and DVDs, and access the internet without getting bogged down. Expect to spend $1,500 to $3,500 on your computer and another $100 to $300 for a high-resolution color display monitor.
- *Printer*. There was a time when your choice of printers was simple: If you wanted to provide quality, you had to have a laser printer. But as inkjet technology improves and prices drop, you may find a lower-priced printer is adequate. You'll likely spend $300 to $1,000 on your printer.

- *Software.* The software you'll need beyond a good word-processing program will depend on the services you offer. Consider a desktop publishing program, photo editing software, presentation software, spreadsheet program, accounting software, and a contact management program. You should be able to get started with the basic Microsoft programs that usually come with a new computer, but you'll soon need additional programs. Expect to spend anywhere from $800 to $2,000 or more on all the software you'll need.
- *Scanner.* You will likely need to scan documents, photographs, and artwork to create electronic files that can be e-mailed or inserted into presentations. Expect to pay $100 to $150 for an adequate scanner.

> **Beware!**
> Only work with legally purchased, properly licensed software, and be sure you read and understand the terms of your software agreement. For example, chances are your software agreement prohibits installation on multiple computers for multiple users unless you pay for that type of use. Law enforcement agencies are cracking down on software piracy; it's better to pay the price and operate legally and ethically than risk criminal charges.

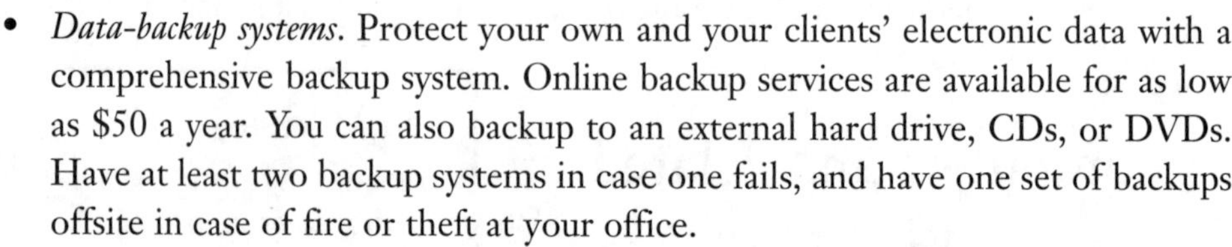

- *Data-backup systems.* Protect your own and your clients' electronic data with a comprehensive backup system. Online backup services are available for as low as $50 a year. You can also backup to an external hard drive, CDs, or DVDs. Have at least two backup systems in case one fails, and have one set of backups offsite in case of fire or theft at your office.
- *Uninterruptible power supply.* To protect your computer system as well as work in progress, all of your machines should be plugged into an uninterruptible power supply that will provide electricity in the event of a power failure. These devices also provide a degree of protection against power surges. Prices range from $50 to $200.
- *Modem.* Modems are necessary to access online services and the internet and have become a standard computer component. For high-speed access, you'll also need a cable, DSL, or ISDN modem. Costs range from $100 to $200 for the modem and $25 to $50 per month for service.

> **Dollar Stretcher**
> Before making a final purchase decision, shop online (both at internet stores and online auction sites such as eBay) as well as at warehouse stores, chain stores, and other suppliers to be sure you're getting the best price, quality, and service package.

Equipment Issues to Consider

On the subject of equipment, there are some issues you need to think about carefully before making the final decision on what to buy, and how to pay for it.

- *Buying used or new.* When buying computers, printers, and other electronic equipment, new is generally the best way to go. Technology is changing so rapidly that used electronics are rarely worth even the discounted price, and reliability can be an issue. Furnishings such as desks, chairs, filing cabinets, and various office fixtures are a different story. These items can safely be purchased used at a substantial savings through dealers, classified ads, and other sources.
- *Service contracts.* In general, service contracts are very expensive insurance policies, and whether or not to purchase them is a judgment call you'll have to make based on the cost of the equipment and of the contract. Consider service contracts in total, not just on a single item. For example, let's say you bought five different service contracts on different items and only one broke down. What was the total you paid for the contracts and what would the repair or replacement have cost had you not had the contract?
- *Lease or buy.* With computers and peripherals becoming increasingly affordable, the leasing option is becoming decreasingly viable. Most leasing companies don't want to bother with a single computer-and-printer package, and business owners find it makes more financial management sense to buy the equipment.

One more thing you need to think about before making your final computer purchase decision is whether to buy a Macintosh or a Windows-based PC. There was a time when Macs were used primarily for graphic design work and didn't have much in the way of other business software available, while Windows (and even the old DOS) systems had plenty of business software but couldn't handle the graphics side as well as Macs. But as both systems have evolved, the differences between them have become more personal preference than capability.

Businesses tend to use Windows-based PCs more than Macintoshes for their basic word-processing and administrative needs. When making your decision, keep in mind that your system needs to be compatible with the majority of your clients' equipment.

Other Office Equipment

- *Photocopier*. The photocopier is a fixture of the modern office and is essential for even the smallest public relations firm. You can get a basic, low-end, no-frills personal copier for less than $400 in just about any office supply store.
- *Fax machine*. Though e-mail has dramatically reduced the number of documents that are faxed, fax machines are still standard equipment in modern offices. For a public relations firm, a stand-alone machine on a dedicated telephone line is a wise investment. Expect to pay $100 to $150 for a fax machine.

> Tip...
>
> **Smart Tip**
>
> Your office library should include a copy of an accepted style guide such as the *Chicago Manual of Style* or the *Associated Press Stylebook* so that your press releases conform to the style standards of the publications you are targeting.

- *Postage scale*. Unless all of your mail is identical, and especially if you are going to be mailing materials for your clients, a postage scale is a valuable investment. An accurate scale takes the guesswork out of postage and will quickly pay for itself. It's a good idea to weigh every piece of mail to eliminate the risk of items being returned for insufficient postage or overpaying when you're unsure of the weight. Light mailers—one to 12 items per day—will be adequately served by inexpensive mechanical postal scales, which typically range from $10 to $25. If you're averaging 12 to 24 items per day, consider a digital scale, which is somewhat more expensive—generally from $45 to $175 (or more for very elaborate units)—but significantly more accurate than a mechanical unit. If you send more than 24 items per day or use priority or expedited services frequently, invest in an electronic computing scale that weighs the item and then calculates the rate via the carrier of your choice, making it easy for you to make comparisons. The availability of a high-quality postage scale can be a competitive advantage if you handle mailings for your clients. Programmable electronic scales range from $70 to $250.
- *Postage meter*. Postage meters allow you to pay for postage in advance and print the exact amount on the mailing piece when it is used. Many postage meters can print in increments of one-tenth of a cent, which can add up to big savings for bulk mail users. Meters also provide a "big company" professional image, are more convenient than stamps, and can save you and your clients money in a number of ways. Postage meters are leased, not sold, with rates starting at about $30 per month. They require a license that is available from your local post office. Only five companies are licensed by the United States Postal

Service to lease postage meters; your local post office can provide you with contact information or you can get details at usps.gov. You can also print postage from your own computer using stamps.com.

- *Paper shredder*. As a response to both a growing concern for privacy and the need to recycle and conserve space in landfills, shredders are becoming increasingly common in both homes and offices. They allow you to efficiently destroy incoming unsolicited direct mail as well as sensitive internal documents and drafts of clients' work before they are discarded. Shredded paper can be compacted much more tightly than paper tossed in a wastebasket, which conserves landfill space. Light-duty shredders start at about $20, and heavier-capacity shredders run $80 to $200.

Bright Idea

Some mailers prefer stamps because they look more personal; others prefer metered mail because it looks more "corporate." Make your decision based on your style and the image you want to create for your company. Suggestion: Use metered mail for invoices, statements, and other official business, and use stamps for thank-you notes and similar marketing correspondence that could use a personal touch.

Telecommunications

The ability to communicate quickly with clients and suppliers is essential to any business. Also, if you have employees who telecommute or if you use homebased independent contractors, being able to reach them quickly is important. Advancing technology gives you a wide range of telecommunications options. Most telephone companies have created departments dedicated to small and homebased businesses. Contact your local service provider and ask to speak with someone who can review your needs and help you put together a service and equipment package that will work for you.

Security

Whether you are homebased or in a commercial location, you need to be sure that your facility is safe and secure for you, your employees, and your clients. And, of course, you also want to protect your equipment, supplies, and any materials belonging to your clients.

Begin by investigating your area's crime history to determine what kind of security measures you need to take. To learn whether your proposed or existing location has a high crime rate, check with the local police department's community relations department or crime prevention officer. Most will gladly provide free information on safeguarding your business and will often personally visit your site to discuss specific crime-prevention strategies. Many also offer training seminars for small businesses and their employees on workplace safety and crime prevention.

The cost of electronic surveillance equipment is dropping and its capabilities are increasing, and installing such security devices may earn you discounts on your insurance. You can also increase the effectiveness of your security system by discreetly posting signs in your windows and around your facility announcing the presence of alarms and cameras.

If you're in a commercial location, be sure the parking lot is well-lit for those times when you or your staffers will be coming and going before dawn and after dark. There will probably be plenty of times when you're on a deadline or dealing with a crisis and you have to work beyond normal business hours. If you are alone in an office late at night, ask the police for extra patrols.

Purchasing

No matter how smart a consumer you are, when it comes to business purchasing, you're playing a whole new game. The rules are different and the stakes significantly higher. But correctly done, purchasing, or procurement, will increase your net income.

Choosing Suppliers

Whether you're buying supplies for your office, a major piece of office equipment, or products or services for your clients, you should evaluate each vendor on quality, service, and price. Look at the product itself as well as the supplementary services and support the company provides.

Verify the company's claims before making a purchase commitment. Ask for references and do a credit check on the vendor. That will tell you how well the supplier pays his own suppliers. If your vendor is not paying his own vendors, he may have trouble getting materials, and that may delay delivery on your order. Or he may simply go out of business without any advance notice, leaving you and your clients in a lurch.

Bright Idea

If you have employees, get their input when making purchasing decisions on supplies and equipment. The people who are using these items every day know best what works and what doesn't, what's efficient and what isn't.

Also confirm the company's general reputation and financial stability by calling the Better Business Bureau, any appropriate licensing agencies, trade associations, and D&B (Dunn & Bradstreet) at dnb.com.

A major component of the purchasing process is the supplier's representative, or salesperson. The knowledge and sophistication level of individual salespeople often

Before You Sign

Contracts are excellent for making sure both supplier and customer are clear on the details of the sale. This is not "just a formality" that can be brushed aside. Read all agreements and support documents carefully, and consider having them reviewed by an attorney. Make sure everything that's important to you (and your clients, if you're purchasing something for them as part of your service) is in writing. Remember, if it's not part of the contract, it's not part of the deal—no matter what the salesperson says. And if it's in the contract, it's probably enforceable, even if the salesperson says that never happens.

Any contract the vendor writes is naturally going to favor the vendor, but you don't have to agree to all the standard boilerplate terms. In addition, you can demand the inclusion of details that are appropriate to your situation. Consider these points when you're negotiating contracts:

- *Make standard provisions apply to both parties.* If, for example, the contract exempts the vendor from specific liabilities, request that the language be revised to exempt you, too.
- *Use precise language.* It's difficult to enforce vague language, so be specific. A clause that states the vendor is not responsible for failures due to "causes beyond the vendor's control" leaves a lot of room for interpretation; more precise language forces a greater level of accountability.
- *Include a "vendor default" provision.* The vendor's contract probably describes the circumstances under which you would be considered to be in default. Include the same protection for yourself.
- *Be wary of vendor representatives who have to get any contract changes approved by "corporate" or some other higher authority.* This is a negotiating technique that generally works against the customer. Insist that the vendor make personnel available who have the authority to negotiate.

depends on the product or industry; however, they can be a tremendous source of education and information. Some businesspeople dismiss sales reps with an attitude of "I don't have time to see peddlers," but this is a mistake. Make it a rule to treat all salespeople with courtesy and respect, but insist that they do the same for you. You can, for example, set and enforce a policy that salespeople are seen only by appointment or at certain hours. You can also ask them in advance how much time you need to allot for your meeting, and stick to that schedule.

Dollar Stretcher

Ask suppliers if payment terms can be a part of your price negotiation. For example, can you get a discount for paying cash in advance?

Besides telling you what they have, salespeople should be asking questions. Just as you do when you're trying to land a new client, a good salesperson will try to find out what your needs are and how his company can satisfy them. Sharp ones may even give you ideas you can take to your clients. As in the consumer sales arena, commercial salespeople use both high- and low-pressure tactics. If you study sales techniques, you'll be able to recognize and respond to the methods being used with you.

Build Strong Supplier Relationships

Reliable suppliers are an asset to your business. They can bail you out when you make an ordering mistake or when your clients make difficult demands on you. But they will do so only as long as your business is profitable to them. Suppliers, like you, are in business to make money. If you argue over every invoice, ask them to shave prices on everything you buy, or fail to pay your bills promptly, don't be surprised when their salespeople stop calling on you or refuse to help you when you're in a bind.

Of course, you want the best deal you can get on a consistent basis from your suppliers. Just keep in mind that no worthwhile business arrangement can continue for long unless something of value is rendered and received by all involved. The best approach is to treat your suppliers the way you would like your clients to treat you.

Find out in advance what your suppliers' credit polices are and pay according to their terms. Many will accept credit cards but will not put you on an open account until they've had a chance to run a credit check on you. They may ask you to provide a financial statement; if they do, don't even think of inflating your numbers to cover a lack of references. This is a felony, and it's easily detected by most credit managers.

If you do open an account with a supplier, be sure you understand the terms and preserve your credit standing by paying on time. Typically, you'll have 30 days to pay, but many companies offer a discount if you pay early.

11

Startup Economics and Setting Fees

An appealing aspect of starting a public relations business is its relatively low startup costs. If you have a decent credit rating, you can be ready to start serving clients with virtually no cash out of pocket—although you'll certainly be on firmer ground if you have some startup capital. The specific equipment you'll need and price ranges have already been discussed. But whether all you have is a credit card or you've got a nice fat savings account ready to invest, opening your doors is only part of the financial picture.

The issue of money has two sides: How much do you need to start and operate, and how much can you expect to take in? Doing this analysis is often extremely difficult for small-business owners who would rather be in the trenches getting the work done than bound to a desk dealing with tiresome numbers.

More than likely, you'll use your personal savings, credit cards, and equipment you already own to get your business up and running. Because the startup costs are relatively low, you'll find traditional financing difficult to obtain. Banks and other lenders would much rather lend amounts significantly larger than you'll need and are likely to be able to qualify for.

Be sure you have enough cash on hand to cover your expenses until the revenue starts coming in. At a minimum, you should have the equivalent of three months' expenses in a savings account to tap if you need it; you'll probably sleep better if you have 6 to 12 months of expenses socked away.

As you're putting together your financial plan, consider these sources of startup funds:

- *Your own resources*. Do a thorough inventory of your assets. People generally have more assets than they immediately realize. They could include savings accounts, equity in real estate, retirement accounts, vehicles, recreation equipment, collections, and other investments. You may opt to sell assets for cash or use them as collateral for a loan. Take a look, too, at your personal line of credit; most of the equipment you'll need is available through retail stores that accept credit cards.
- *Friends and family*. The logical next step after gathering your own resources is to approach friends and relatives who believe in you and want to help you succeed. Be cautious with these arrangements; no matter how close you are, present yourself professionally, put everything in writing, and be sure the individuals you approach can afford to take the risk of investing in your business.
- *Partners*. Consider using the "strength in numbers" principle and look around for someone who may want to team up with you in your venture. You may choose

Tip...

Smart Tip

Most of the equipment you need can be purchased at a retail store and charged on a credit card, but too much debt can doom your business before it gets off the ground. Only use your credit cards for items that will contribute to revenue generation, and have a repayment plan in place before you buy.

How Much Do You Need?

So what do you need in the way of cash and available credit to open your doors? Depending on what you already own, the services you want to offer, and whether you'll be homebased or in a commercial location, that number could range from a few hundred to thousands of dollars.

That's where a solid business plan comes in. As you consider your own situation, don't pull a startup number out of the air; use your business plan to calculate how much you need to start your ideal operation, and then figure out how much you have. If you have all the cash you need, you're very fortunate. If you don't, you need to start playing with the numbers and deciding what you can do without.

someone who has financial resources and wants to work side-by-side with you in the business. Or you may find someone who has money to invest but no interest in doing the actual work. Be sure to create a written partnership agreement that clearly defines your respective responsibilities and obligations.

- *Government programs.* Take advantage of the abundance of local, state, and federal programs designed to support small businesses. Make your first stop the U.S. Small Business Administration; then investigate various other programs. Women, minorities, and veterans should check out niche financing possibilities designed to help these groups get into business. The business section of your local library is a good place to begin your research.

Pricing PR Services

There are a number of ways you can charge for your services: hourly, retainer, per project, or by results. Finding the perfect rate that isn't too low or too high can be a challenge for a new PR business. If you're going to have a successful, profitable company, you can't price yourself too low. On the other hand, it would be equally unwise to price yourself higher than what your market is willing and able to pay.

Pricing can be tedious and time-consuming, particularly if you don't have a knack for juggling numbers. Especially in the beginning, don't rush through this process. You need to consider a number of factors including:

- *Overhead.* This includes the various costs involved in operating your business, such as rent/mortgage, payroll, insurance, taxes, advertising, debt service, utilities, professional services such as accountants and attorneys, telephone, office supplies, and so on.
- *Desired income.* How much income do you want to be able to take out of the business? Depending on your structure, this would be either your salary or the business's net profit.
- *Capacity.* How much time can you reasonably expect to be working for clients? Another way to think of this is to figure out how many billable hours will you have? Remember that the time you need to spend doing administrative tasks is not billable.

Calculate your monthly overhead. Some items, such as insurance premiums, may be paid once or twice a year, so you need to pro-rate those items to get a per month cost and factor them into your figures. Then add on your desired income or profit. Divide that by the number of billable hours you have in a month, and you have an hourly rate baseline. This number can guide what you charge when working by the hour, and serve as the basis when developing retainer and project fees.

When you set up a client on a retainer, your contract should clearly stipulate what the retainer covers, whether it's a specific number of hours or a predetermined set of professional services. You should also be clear on what happens if the client does not use the full amount of allotted services or time (will he simply lose it or will you roll it over into the next month?) and what you'll charge if you have to exceed the amount of work covered by the retainer (will you charge an hourly rate or deduct that work from the following month?). Typically, retainers are paid in advance and hourly projects are paid in arrears. Terms on project rates are negotiable. Depending on the size of the project, the client may make payments in installments, beginning with an advance followed by payments at specified points in the process.

Many public relations firms include their fee structures on their websites, so it's fairly easy for you to get an idea of what the going rate is for

Tip...

Smart Tip

If the client says your quote is too high, consider taking away services to bring the price down—don't just lower the fee. Reducing your rates without any concession from the client says you didn't feel you were worth what you wanted to charge in the first place.

various services. Whether or not you choose to publish your rates is a decision only you can make.

Bright Idea

Remind your clients that the cost of a strong public relations effort is not an expense, it's an investment that should result in increased sales.

Pay for Results

A number of public relations firms have adopted a pay-for-performance billing model, typically built around charging for successful media placements. While this may seem like a good idea to clients, it has its drawbacks. One is that it's impossible to guarantee media coverage. Another is that public relations involve far more than simply mentions in articles or on radio and television.

Educate your clients to the fact that one media hit, even a big one, may or may not have the desired impact. That's just publicity. The real value in effective public relations is through an ongoing strategic program that includes publicity and a broad range of other elements.

Of course, your clients are entitled to results for their investment with you, which is why you should always monitor and measure the results of your work, as discussed in Chapter 5.

Expenses

It's common for PR agencies to add expenses onto their fees, billing those charges either at cost or with a standard agency markup, typically ranging from 17 to 20 percent. Expenses could include such items as travel, postage, courier, and communications, as well as specific items purchased for your clients, including printing, photography, art, research, and production costs.

Bright Idea

If you're working too much and can't afford to cut back because you need the money, raise your rates. You might lose a few clients, but they're the ones for whom price is more important than quality and results. Reasonable clients expect periodic rate increases.

12

Assembling Your Team

You can choose to start and run a successful public relations firm as a one-person show, but to really grow, you're going to need employees. If you find the idea of interviewing, hiring, and managing employees somewhat intimidating, you're not alone. That's a common feeling among entrepreneurs. But this is very much a people business. The people you hire will be critical to the success of your company, so it's in your best interest to do it carefully and wisely.

It's a good idea to hire people before you desperately need them. Waiting until the last minute may drive you to make hiring mistakes, which can cost you dearly, both in terms of cash and customer service.

When you first begin hiring people, you may want to consider bringing them on as part-timers until your business grows to the point at which full-timers are required. One of the biggest keys to getting and keeping good people is flexibility, and you will find plenty of talented folks who, for whatever reason, don't want to work full time. If you can accommodate them, you'll both benefit. And as the workload grows and you need a full-time person doing that particular job, either change the status of your part-timer or, if that won't work, be creative. Consider hiring a second part-timer, setting up a job-sharing situation, or finding some other solution that will allow you to retain a valuable person and still get the work done.

Hiring Steps

The first step in formulating a comprehensive human resources program is to decide exactly what you want someone to do. The job description doesn't have to be as formal as one you might expect from a large corporation, but it needs to clearly outline the person's duties and responsibilities: writing press releases, doing research, contacting media, managing projects, and so on. It should also list any special skills or other required credentials, such as technical skills for someone working in the area of online public relations or a valid driver's license for someone who is going to need to drive in the course of the job.

Next, establish pay scales. Rates vary by geographic location and the skills required. You can get a good idea of the pay ranges in your area simply by checking the classified ads in your local paper. You can also compare salary ranges in your area with those in other parts of the country by going to salary.com. To find out national average pay scales for a variety of positions, go to the website for the U.S. Department of Labor, Bureau of Labor Statistics at bls.gov.

Beware!

Before you hire your first employee, make sure you are prepared. Have all your paperwork ready, know what you need to do in the way of tax reporting and understand all of the liabilities and responsibilities that come with having employees.

You'll also need a job application form. You can get a basic form at most office supply stores or you can create your own. Have your

Before You Hire

Before you set up the first interview with an applicant, there are things you should do to make the hiring process as smooth as possible.

- *Decide in advance what you need.* You know you need help, but exactly what kind of help? Do you need an account manager or administrative support? In the very beginning, you'll be looking for people to do the tasks you can't or don't want to do. As you grow, you'll be looking for people who can help you expand your capabilities.
- *Write job descriptions.* Take the time to put a list of responsibilities and required skills in writing. This forces you to think through what type of person will best meet your needs, which reduces the risk of hiring the wrong person. It also gives you something to show an applicant, so she can tell if the job you are offering is the one she wants.
- *Set basic personnel policies.* Don't think that because you're a small company, you can just deal with personnel issues as they come up. You'll avoid a lot of problems down the road if you set policies in advance.

attorney review the form you'll be using for compliance with the most current employment laws.

Every prospective employee should fill out an application, even if it's someone you know and even if he has submitted a detailed resume. A resume is not a signed, sworn statement acknowledging that you can fire the person if he lies; an application is. The application will also help you verify his resume; compare the two and make sure the information is consistent.

Now you're ready to start looking for candidates.

Where to Look

A successful hiring search will go beyond just writing a help-wanted ad and posting the job in the local paper or on an online employment website. Sources for prospective employees include suppliers, former co-workers, clients, and professional associations. Check with nearby colleges for part-time help. Put the word out among your social contacts as well. You never know who might know the perfect person for your operation.

Use caution if you decide to hire friends and relatives. Many personal relationships are not strong enough to survive an employee-employer situation. Small-business owners in all industries tell of nightmarish experiences when a friend or relative refused to accept direction or in other ways abused a personal relationship in the course of business.

The key to success as an employer is making it clear from the start that you are the one in charge. You don't need to act like a dictator, of course. Be diplomatic, but set the ground rules in advance and stick to them.

Evaluating Applicants

When you actually begin the hiring process, don't be surprised if you're as nervous at the prospect of interviewing potential employees as they are about being interviewed. After all, they may need a job, but the future of your company is at stake.

It's a good idea to prepare your interview questions in advance. Develop open-ended questions that encourage the candidate to talk. In addition to knowing *what* they've done, you want to find out *how* they did it. You might even ask them to tell you how they would handle specific situations they're likely to face while working for you. For example, ask prospective account managers how they would handle a new product launch or what they would do if a client got arrested. Ask each candidate for a particular position the same set of questions, and take notes as they respond so you can make an accurate assessment and comparison later.

When the interview is over, let the candidate know what to expect. Is it going to take you several weeks to interview other candidates, check references, and make a decision? Will you want the top candidates to return for a second interview? Will you call the candidates, or should they call you? This is not only a good business practice; it's also just simple common courtesy.

Always check former employers and personal references. Though many companies are very restrictive as to what information they'll verify, you may be surprised at what you can find out. Certainly you should at least confirm that the applicant told the truth about dates and positions held. Personal references are likely to give you some additional insight into the general character and personality of the candidate; this will help you decide if he'll fit into your operation.

Be sure to document every step of the interview and reference-checking process. Even very small companies are finding themselves targets of employment discrimination suits; if it happens to you, good records are your best defense.

Background Checks

Screen your employees carefully. Negligent or dishonest employees can harm your clients, damage your reputation, and be the cause of lawsuits.

Don't try to conduct background checks yourself. This is a task best left to an expert. Expect to pay anywhere from $50 to $200 for a professional background check, depending on how much detail you need. Check your telephone directory under "investigative services" to find a resource for background checks, or ask other business owners for a referral.

Let applicants know you will be conducting a background check to verify all of their answers. Though it is unlikely that many people will admit to a history of adverse conduct—although it's likely you will be surprised and even shocked by what job applicants will tell you—it is possible that the attention you direct to the issue will discourage someone with a

Beware!

Sometimes small companies lose good employees to larger firms that have better career opportunities. They may not be attracted as much by the money and benefits as they are by the room to grow and advance. Do the best you can to offer career growth to your people, but understand that it may not be enough and there isn't much you can do about it.

Check for Eligibility

Under the Immigration Reform and Control Act of 1986, you may only hire people who may legally work in the United States, which means citizens and nationals of the United States, and aliens authorized to work in the United States. As an employer, you must verify the identity and employment eligibility of everyone you hire. You must complete and retain the employment Eligibility Verification Form (I-9) on file for at least three years, or one year after employment ends, whichever period of time is longer.

The Immigration and Nationality Act protects U.S. citizens and aliens authorized to accept employment in the United States from discrimination in hiring or discharge on the basis of national origin and citizenship status.

shady past from seeking employment with your firm. Many will not even bother to fill out an application or take the time for an interview if they know they can't pass the background check.

Employees or Independent Contractors?

An important part of the hiring process is deciding whether you want to hire employees of your own or go with independent contractors. There are advantages and disadvantages to both approaches. What's important is that you clearly understand the difference so you can avoid unnecessary and costly mistakes at tax time.

As an employer, you have greater control over employees than you do over independent contractors. Employees must comply with company policies and with instructions and direction they receive from you or a manager. You can set their hours and other conditions of employment, along with their compensation package. Of course, you must also pay payroll taxes, workers' compensation insurance, unemployment benefits, and any other employee benefits you may decide to offer.

If you use independent contractors, you should have a written agreement that gives a detailed description of the services the worker is to perform, the anticipated time frame within which they are to carry out those duties, and how much they will be paid. The agreement can also be instrumental in confirming that the person is, indeed, an independent contractor and not a salaried employee in the event the IRS or any other agency questions the working relationship. For more information, consult your accountant or tax advisor, or see Publication 15-A, *Employers Supplemental Tax Guide*, which is available from the IRS.

Bright Idea

Call local law firms and ask if they offer free newsletters or seminars on employment law or other issues that affect your operation. Most will be happy to add you to their mailing list at no charge.

Correctly classifying workers is important, and failing to do so can result in severe penalties. The fine for an intentional misclassification can be a penalty equal to 100 percent of the amount of taxes owed. The IRS is very aggressive about payroll taxes, and audits can be triggered by disgruntled former contract employees who feel they have been misclassified and decide to file a complaint.

Hiring Older Employees

The traditional picture of retirement is changing dramatically. Increasingly, retirees are rejecting the idea of collecting the gold watch and spending their final years rocking on the porch. They're active, they're busy, and many are continuing to work. Lifting the Social Security earnings cap has strengthened the senior labor pool and provided businesses in all industries with an excellent source of staffing. As employees, seniors bring a plethora of experience, knowledge, expertise, and ability to the workplace. They tend to provide a higher level of customer service than their younger counterparts and often have experience that will help you with the overall management of the operation.

Seniors are likely to stay with you longer than the worker just beginning a career. A 65-year-old who finds a job in which he likes the environment, the management, and the people he works with is more likely to stay with you long term, say for another 10 years, until the point when he can no longer function efficiently enough to do the job, than a 22-year-old who is going to be looking almost every moment for that job change and the opportunity to move to the next step. Another benefit of hiring seniors is that many have their health insurance and retirement plans in place, which saves you the cost of providing these benefits.

> Tip...
>
> **Smart Tip**
>
> From the day they are hired, tell employees what they need to do to get a raise without having to ask for it. Then follow-up by increasing their pay rates when they've earned it.

Accommodate whatever physical limitations senior employees have as much as possible. If you notice a physical deterioration, communicate your concerns before it becomes a serious problem and work with the employee to make adjustments in his duties if appropriate. Of course, if the worker's declining physical condition gets to the point that he can't do the work, you must terminate his employment. Do that with as much kindness, compassion, and support as possible.

Once They're on Board

The hiring process is only the beginning of the challenge of having employees. You need to provide a thorough and immediate orientation for new employees. Many small businesses conduct their "training" just by throwing someone into the job.

That's not fair to the employee, and it's certainly not good for your business. If you think you can't afford to spend time on training, think again—can you afford *not* to adequately train your employees? Do you really want them taking care of your clients without knowing exactly what to do?

Whether done in a formal classroom setting or on the job, effective training begins with a clear goal and a plan for reaching it. Training falls into one of three major categories: orientation, which includes explaining company policies and procedures; job skills, which focuses on how to do specific tasks; and ongoing development, which enhances the basic job skills and grooms employees for future challenges and opportunities. These tips will help you maximize your training efforts:

- *Find out how people learn best.* Delivering training is not a one-size-fits-all proposition. People absorb and process information differently, and your training method needs to be compatible with their individual preferences. Some people can read a manual, others prefer a verbal explanation, and still others need to see a demonstration.
- *Be a strong role model.* Don't expect more from your employees than you are willing to do. You're a good role model when you do things the way they should be done all the time. Don't take shortcuts you don't want your employees to take or behave in any way you don't want them to behave. On the other hand, don't assume that simply doing things the right way is enough to teach others how to do things. Role-modeling is not a substitute for training; it reinforces training. If you only role-model but never train, employees aren't likely to get the message.
- *Look for training opportunities.* Once you get beyond basic orientation and job skills training, you need to be constantly on the lookout for opportunities to enhance the skill and performance levels of your people.
- *Make it real.* Whenever possible, use real-life situations to train, but avoid letting your clients know they've become a training experience for employees.
- *Anticipate questions.* Don't assume that employees know what to ask. In a new situation, people often don't understand enough to formulate questions. Anticipate their questions and answer them in advance.

Bright Idea

Find out what your employees want in the way of benefits before you spend time and money developing a package. Do a brief survey; ask what they think of the ideas you have, and what ideas they have. If they want something you can't afford to do, don't reject it immediately. Figure out what you *can* afford, and explain the situation to the employee.

- *Ask for feedback.* Finally, encourage employees to let you know how you're doing as a trainer. Just as you evaluate their performance, convince them that it's OK to tell you the truth, ask them what they thought of the training and your techniques, and use that information to improve your own training skills.

Employee Benefits

The actual wages you pay may be only part of your employees' total compensation. While many very small companies do not offer a formal benefits program, more and more business owners have recognized that benefits, particularly in the area of insurance, are extremely important when it comes to attracting and retaining quality employees.

Typical benefits packages include group insurance (your employees may pay all or a portion of their premiums), paid holidays, and vacations. Some businesses offer year-end bonuses based on the company's profitability. You can build employee loyalty by seeking additional benefits that may be somewhat unusual, and they don't have to cost much. Some ideas to consider include paying for memberships to warehouse clubs such as Costco or Sam's; bringing in breakfast or lunch periodically (always with some notice, so that employees can plan); paying for professional association dues and trade journal subscriptions; and contributing to the cost of continuing education. Many employees view telecommuting as a tremendous benefit, so if your employees can effectively work from home part of the time, consider allowing it.

Bright Idea

If you have employees, consider using a payroll service rather than trying to handle this task yourself. The service will calculate taxes; handle reporting and paying local, state, and federal payroll taxes; make deductions for savings, insurance premiums, and loan payments; and may offer other benefits to you and your employees.

Same-Sex Marriages and Employee Benefits

One of the hottest political topics these days is the issue of same-sex marriages. While many people are quick to offer an opinion on the subject, what is not clear is the impact on the areas of employment and employee benefits of a state allowing same-sex marriages.

At the present, federal law, which dominates the area of employee benefits, does not recognize same-sex marriage. This means employers cannot be compelled to treat same-sex spouses in the same manner as opposite-sex spouses for purposes of benefits governed by the Employee Retirement Income Security Act (ERISA).

However, there are certain areas in which state law and the recognition of same-sex marriage may have an impact. An employer generally may extend benefits to individuals including spouses under same-sex marriages, even where not required by law.

Your best strategy is to understand the issues related to same-sex marriage and employee benefits; decide on an overall approach to dealing with same-sex marriage; be sure that approach is clearly defined in your policies and consistently applied; and review and revise your benefit plans and employment practices as necessary.

Personnel Files

Maintaining complete and current personnel files is an important part of your business administration. Store these documents in a secure place such as a locked filing cabinet, and limit who has access to them.

Personnel files are used to make job-related decisions affecting employees, and, therefore, should contain only information that can be legally used in making those decisions. Because federal and state law prohibits the use of sex, race, national origin, color, religion, disability, or veteran's status to make employment decisions, documents contain this information should not be included in personnel files. Similarly, medical information, garnishment orders and records, and I-9 documents should be filed separately from the employee's primary personnel file.

The personnel information you maintain on each employee should include:

- The signed and dated employment application, resume, and other hiring records.
- Basic employee information: name, address, Social Security number, date of birth, job classification, I-9, work permits for minors.
- A copy of your offer of employment.
- All employment actions, including hires, separations, rehires, promotions, demotions, transfers, layoffs, and recalls.
- A current photo of the employee that you update annually. This does not need to be a portrait; a snapshot taken with an instant or digital camera is sufficient.
- Copies of any pre-employment testing, including drug test results.
- Copies of all special qualifications, including licenses and certifications.

- Records of any training the employee completes after coming on board.
- Copies of performance reviews, commendations, and discipline or other corrective action notices.
- Payroll information.
- Records of any job-related illnesses and injuries.
- Home address, telephone number, and emergency contact information.
- For employees who drive as part of their job, a copy of current, valid driver's license; for employees who use their own vehicle on the job, a copy of current insurance certificate.

Noncompete and Confidentiality Agreements

It is likely that your employees will learn information about your company and your clients that could be damaging in the hands of a competitor. Also, workers in the public relations industry are often mobile and may try to take clients with them when they change jobs.

By signing a noncompete agreement, an employee promises not to work for a direct competitor for a specific time after he leaves your company. Your agreement may also include restrictions on employees starting their own businesses that would directly compete with yours. You may also want to ask employees to sign confidentiality agreements that would prevent them from disclosing sensitive business information or trade secrets—either of yours or your clients—to competitors.

Noncompete agreements can be difficult to enforce, especially if they are extremely restrictive. The legal system puts value on a person's right to earn a living. If you are considering setting a policy that would require noncompete and confidentiality agreements, check with an employment attorney to make sure what you want to do is legal in your state and that the agreement will stand up in court.

13

Financial Management

One of the primary indicators of the overall health of your business is its financial status, and it's important that you monitor your financial progress closely. The only way you can do that is to keep good records. You can handle the process manually or use any of the excellent computer accounting software programs on the market. You might want to ask your accountant for assistance getting your system set up. The key is to get set up correctly at the start and keep your records current and accurate throughout the life of your company.

Keeping good records helps generate financial statements that tell you exactly where you stand and what you need to do next. The key financial statements you need to understand and use regularly are:

- *Profit and loss statement.* Also called the P&L or the income statement, it illustrates how much your company is making or losing over a designated period—monthly, quarterly, or annually—by subtracting expenses from revenue to arrive at a net result, which is either a profit or a loss.
- *Balance sheet.* A table showing your assets, liabilities, and capital at a specific point. A balance sheet is typically generated monthly, quarterly, or annually when the books are closed.
- *Cash flow statement.* Summarizes the operating, investing, and financing activities of your business as they relate to the inflow and outflow of cash. As with the profit and loss statement, a cash flow statement is prepared to reflect a specific accounting period, such as monthly, quarterly, or annually.

Successful PR-business owners review these reports regularly—at least monthly—so they always know where they stand and can quickly move to correct minor difficulties before they become major financial problems. If you wait until November to figure out whether or not you made a profit in February, you won't be in business for long. But monitoring your financial progress takes discipline, particularly when you're growing fast and working hard. If you don't do it, you'll find yourself at the end of the year with nothing to show for your hard work and not knowing how to improve your profitability the following year. You need to know which clients and which types of projects make you money—and which don't.

Setting Credit Policies

When you extend credit to someone, you are essentially providing them with an interest-free loan. You wouldn't expect someone to lend you money without getting information from you about where you live and work, and your ability to repay. It just makes sense that you would want to get this information from someone to whom you are lending money.

Reputable companies will not object to providing you with credit information and to paying you before you begin working according to your contract. If you're not comfortable asking for at least part of the money upfront, just think how you'll feel if you do a lot of work for a client and don't get paid at all. You might find it difficult to ask for advance payment and to insist on a complete, signed credit application along with a personal guarantee from the client company's owner—until the first time you get burned. Then it will be easy.

> **Bright Idea**
>
> Photocopy checks before depositing them. That way, if a collection problem occurs later, you have the client's current bank information in your files, and that makes collecting on a judgment much easier.

Your credit policy should address how far an account may be in arrears before you suspend services until the account is paid in full. This is always a tough call, because it's easy to get emotionally invested in your clients. Just remember that you are a for-profit business, and if you don't get paid, you can't pay your own bills and make a profit.

Your credit policy should include a clear collection strategy. Do not ignore overdue bills; the older a bill gets, the less likely it will ever be paid. Be prepared to take action on past-due accounts as soon as they become past due.

Billing

Establish and follow sound billing procedures from the beginning. Be clear and consistent, so your clients aren't surprised or confused. When you can, coordinate your billing system with your clients' payable procedures. Candidly ask what you can do to ensure prompt payment; that may include confirming the correct billing address and finding out what documentation is required to help the client confirm the validity of the invoice. Keep in mind that many large companies pay certain types of invoices on certain days of the month; find out if your clients do that, and schedule your invoices to arrive in time for the next payment cycle.

> **Beware!**
>
> There may be times when you'll need to make special purchases (such as equipment, software, or supplies) to handle a particular project for a client. Before you invest in a project, be sure you will get the work. If a project requires an investment in training, staffing, or equipment, it's not unreasonable to insist on a contract and advance payment before you begin.

Most computer bookkeeping software programs include basic invoices. If you design your own invoices and statements, be sure they're clear and easy to understand. Detail each item, and indicate the amount due in bold with the words "Please pay" in front of the total. A confusing invoice may get set aside for clarification, and your payment will be delayed. Bill your work according to the terms of the contract, whether that's monthly, at the completion of a project, or under some other arrangement.

Check then Recheck

Just because a client passed your first credit check with flying colors doesn't mean you should never re-evaluate their credit status. In fact, you should do it on a regular basis.

Tell customers when you initially grant their credit application that you have a policy of periodically reviewing accounts so that when you do, it's not a surprise. Remember, things can change very quickly in the business world, and a company that is on sound financial footing this year may be quite wobbly next year. You might think the nature of your work would give you a clue if this happens. It should, but it might not. Some key trouble signs are a slowdown in payments, unusual complaints about the quality of your work that you weren't getting before, and difficulty getting answers to your payment inquiries.

Take the same approach to a credit review as you do to a new credit application. Most of the time, you can use what you have on file to conduct the check, but if you're concerned for any reason, you may want to ask the client for updated information.

Most clients will understand routine credit reviews and accept them as a sound business practice. A client who objects may well have something to hide, and that's something you need to know.

Accepting Credit and Debit Cards

Accepting credit cards is not as common in the public relations business as it is in other industries, such as retail and restaurant. For firms that do a substantial amount of their business online, such as some of the pay-for-results and press release distribution services, it makes sense to accept credit cards. Some small clients may appreciate being able to pay by credit card as a cash flow management tool and to benefit

Tip...

Smart Tip

You want to make a good impression when applying for a loan. That includes presenting your company's materials in a businesslike manner. Assemble and organize all of your paperwork in a professional folder or portfolio, along with any relevant brochures and price lists.

Ask Before You Need

Just about every growing business experiences economic rough spots and requires financing of some type sooner or later. Plan for the costs of growth and watch for signs of developing problems so you can figure out how to best deal with them before they turn into a major crisis.

Asking for money before you need it is especially important if you're going to be applying for a loan, whether it's from a private individual or a commercial loan source such as your bank. Most lenders are understandably reluctant to extend credit to a business in trouble. So plan your growth and presell your banker on your financial needs. Such foresight demonstrates that you are an astute professional manager on top of every situation. Your chances of obtaining the funding you need will improve significantly.

from special deals the credit card company offers. But most PR firms can operate successfully without accepting credit and debit cards.

You may still decide you want to be able to offer this payment option. It's much easier now to get merchant status than it has been in the past; in fact, these days merchant status providers are competing aggressively for your business. You'll begin receiving sales pitches as soon as you file the paperwork to create your company.

To get a credit card merchant account, start with your own bank. Also check with various professional associations that offer merchant status as a member benefit. Shop around; this is a competitive industry, and it's worth taking the time to get the best deal.

Cash Management: Don't Pay Before You Have To

One of the most overlooked capital-raising techniques is doing a better job of managing the cash you have. As obvious as the concept of efficient cash management may seem, it's often neglected because business owners underestimate how valuable it can be.

One key area of cash management is holding on to your money as long as possible by slowing down disbursements legally and fairly. For example, if an invoice is due on the 15th and you pay it on the 5th, you're losing use of those funds for 10 days and getting nothing in return.

The bottom line is not to pay anything before you have to. Even though you may have a system where you process payables on certain days, hold the checks and don't mail them until they are due. Or use electronic payment systems to make payments on the date they are due.

You may also be able to negotiate longer payment terms with certain creditors. This amounts to an interest-free loan from vendors. Communicate your needs clearly; let vendors know how they will benefit by helping you, perhaps with larger orders in the future; then be sure to honor whatever terms you agree to.

However, waiting until the last minute to pay is not always the best strategy. When negotiating terms, consider the value of early-payment discounts. If the discount is greater than your cost of borrowing money, you'll save money by paying early.

If you have a revolving line of credit, talk to your banker about setting up a "sweep" account. This means the bank will automatically apply whatever cash you have on hand at the end of each day to reduce the balance—and therefore the interest—on your loan. When checks are presented for payment, the amount is charged to your line of credit.

The Bottom Line

You are probably attracted to the public relations industry because you find the work appealing and you want to be in business for yourself because you have an entrepreneurial spirit. Remember that to stay in business, you must be profitable. Even though it might not be as much fun as developing an exciting PR plan for a client, discipline yourself to manage the financial side of your company. That's the only way you'll be able to enjoy the long-term fruits of your labors.

Appendix A
Marketing Your Business

The information in this section will help you as you market your own firm as well as when you work with your clients to make public relations a part of their marketing strategy. Much of the information you gather and need to understand to develop a marketing plan will also be useful as you plan an effective public relations strategy, whether it's for your own firm or your clients. No matter how successful you become, you can always benefit from understanding and using strong sales skills.

MARKETING PLAN OVERVIEW

Business owners and executives today tend to be less focused on marketing plans than on tactics such as internet advertising, sales brochures, and Flash animation. And although these devices are legitimate tools of the trade, they become temporary, patchwork fixes when substituted for implementing a well-thought-out plan. Invariably the work is OK for a while, but over time companies run by these managers often get crushed under the weight of competition and go under.

As a matter of fact, a 2003 U.S. Department of Commerce research study concluded that more than 80 percent of American companies of all sizes experience lower-than-anticipated marketing activity results and the vast majority of these do not have written marketing plans! This is not a coincidental relationship.

A marketing plan is a written roadmap that documents a company's short and/or long-term objectives, the strategies and actions necessary to achieve them, and the relevant data used to support these forecasts and conclusions. Among other things it includes a business's:

- Vision and mission
- Product and service offerings
- Target audience
- Pricing policies
- Sales, revenue, and profitability forecasts
- Distribution channels
- Communication strategies

Traditionally, marketing plans covered at least three yeas, but modern businesses increasingly opt for shorter cycles, which we recommend. In any case, the plan should be updated yearly. It can be for a single product, service, brand, or an entire product line. Simply put, its goal is to bring strategies to life and, as former Giants quarterback Fran Tarkinton said, "wrestle that bear to the ground."

What Is a Marketing Plan NOT

Although it should be a large part of a full-blown business plan, it is not a substitute for one. Business plans contain additional information, such as:

- Sources of funding
- Capital equipment lists
- Balance sheets
- Historical financial reports
- Copies of legal documents
- Income statements

Moreover, a business plan contains more detailed information on a company's resources, day-to-day management, operational activities, and capital investments, all of which either feed into, or from, the marketing process.

The Truth About Marketing Plans

A marketing plan is not rocket science. A marketing plan is not at all similar to a Ph.D. dissertation. A marketing plan can be handwritten, and it can have typos. A markting plan can be created with crayons. A marketing plan can be developed by anyone, as long as they can follow a simple recipe. Writing a marketing plan may not be your idea of fun, but spending more time with family and friends, and enjoying the extra money you'll make (because you wrote it and it worked), is loads of fun. A marketing plan will help you save money and make money. A marketing plan means fewer headaches. A marketing plan is a vital, living document that can be dog-eared, written on, and highlighted. A marketing plan saves time, no matter how long it takes to write. A marketing plan has to-do lists and not-to-do lists. A marketing plan is your guide, your sanity check, your blueprint, your roadmap, and your business's best friend.

Good Reasons for Writing a Marketing Plan

The single best reason for writing a marketing plan is in the journey, not the plan. In other words, in order to end up at the final destination (i.e., the written plan) its author(s) must conduct relevant research; assess their own strengths and weaknesses; define their goals; set measurement standards, and the like. Thus the process itself will provide you invaluable insights and incredible peace of mind.

Additionally, they're undertaken to:

- Set objectives as part of a yearly planning process;
- Assess the viability of new business ventures;
- Be included in an overall business plan, especially when a company is seeking investment capital;
- Introduce a new product; enter a new market; and/or grow an existing product or service line;
- Document specific, additional strategies for new products, projects, programs, market areas, etc.

Most importantly, however, they provide business people with far better odds of achieving their goals. If you don't have goals, you don't need a marketing plan!

So, what do you hope to accomplish by writing your marketing plan? Please enter your answer in the space below.

I am (we are) writing this marketing plan in order to:

____

____

____

____

____

Goal Attainment = Inputs + Processes

Once you have defined your purpose, in order to enjoy the journey and make the effort worthwhile, evaluate what you have to do to achieve it. As the saying goes, "Junk in, junk out" (a variation of GIGO). Simply put, your ability to achieve any purpose hinges on two things:

1. *Inputs*. The ingredients you use. In this case, they are your resources and assets, such as time, money, people, machines, and raw materials.
2. *Processes*. These are the systematized actions—decisions, tasks, behaviors, planning, brainstorming, purchasing, writing, and the like—you'll perform to complete the job.

Do not forget these—write them down on a Post-It™ note, tape them written backwards on your forehead, pin them on a bulletin board, make them your screen saver.

The integrity of your marketing plan, which will play a large part in achieving your goals, depends upon the quality of your inputs and processes. That's why you should continually question and assess them to ensure that you're maximizing your chances for success.

One of the best ways to do this is by developing systems, the bridges that connect your available resources (inputs) to your goal. Systems are really just standardized methods for solving problems. When they work well, you achieve predictable results. If not, your results will be disappointing.

Here's a straightforward analogy:

Let's assume our friend, Lucy, is hosting an informal dinner party for twelve of her friends on Sunday. After some thought, she decides to serve wild rice soup; although she's never made it before, she understands that it's delicious and a perfect solution for small gatherings. Additionally, Lucy feels confident that she'll end up with a big pot of warm, scrumptious, and creamy soup for her friends.

So, in this case the following apply:

1. *The goal*: to make enough warm, scrumptious, creamy wild rice soup to serve herself and 12 others by Sunday at 2 P.M.
2. *The inputs*
   - *The recipe*. This defines much of the process she'll use to make her soup.
   - *The ingredients*. 7 cups of cooked wild rice, 2 sticks of butter, 3.5 cups half-and-half, 2-3 grated carrots, two onions, one ham steak, 10 tsp. slivered almonds.
   - *Time requirements*. Half hour for preparation; 1 hr. for cooking.
   - *Equipment*. A large pot, functioning stove, 13 bowls, 13 spoons.
   - *Labor*. Someone to prepare the soup, or Lucy.

Lack of any of these inputs will have a direct, and negative, effect on Lucy's ability to achieve her goal—some more than others. For instance, if she uses one onion instead of two, the impact would be negligible. Conversely, however, if Lucy doesn't have a stove, and can't use someone else's or come up with an alternative such as a grill, she's dead in the water. She'd either have to change her menu (how about gazpacho?) or figure out another way to heat her soup.

Once she is convinced that she probably has, or can purchase, the necessary equipment, Lucy does the smart thing and asks her chef friend for his favorite wild rice soup recipe, and voila! she's ready to go.

Now Lucy just has to assess which ingredients she already has and which she'll have to purchase, and make sure she understands all the steps involved, or:

3. *The process*. The actions she'll use to complete the job, such as:
   - Making a list of ingredients she needs to purchase.
   - Traveling to and from the grocery store, selecting and paying for what she needs.
   - Reading and following the directions on her recipe.

Lucy's ability to attain her goal depends on a number of different variables such as the quality of the directions she receives; how well she interprets them, and/or her ability to measure the ingredients accurately.

Every time she deviates from the system and compromises the inputs or process—overcooks the rice, fails to double the recipe, or worse, ditches the recipe and decides to "wing it"—she increase the chances that her soup, or output, will not live up to her expectations. In any case, she'll achieve a result (soup) but not necessarily her goal (warm, creamy, scrumptious wild rice soup for 13). So Lucy needs not only inputs and processes, but also a valid system if she wants to achieve reliable results.

If Lucy ignores the trial-and-error practice and knowledge used to create the recipe and decides to go it alone, she's far more likely to overlook essential inputs and ignore vital processes. And, as they say, the proof is in the pudding (or soup).

Results vs. Goals: The Good, the Bad, and the So-So

Whenever you input resources and complete a series of related actions (processes)—ones with a beginning, middle, and end—you will get results, or "R."

The challenge lies in doing everything in your power to ensure that your Rs meet or exceed your goals, or Gs!

If R > G, you've managed to exceed your expectations.

If R = G, you've hit the nail on the head.

If R< G, you fell short of your goal.

Our soup analogy aptly demonstrates how these variances can occur, but keep in mind that this uncomplicated example illustrates the concept in its most primitive form. In this instance, Lucy had only one very specific goal that could be completed quickly, inexpensively, and without a great deal of planning.

But what if it were more involved? What if Lucy's ultimate goal was to open a wild rice soup catering business and she was preparing this one pot of soup in an attempt to perfect her recipe? If so, she did not achieve her longer term goal, no matter how her soup turned out.

Rather, her result, or sub-goal, either got her one step closer to her big "G" and she could check the recipe off her list and begin working on other sub-goals such as, looking into a business license, obtaining funding, or finding a location; or it's back to the drawing board for our friend. You get the idea.

And even if Lucy's soup is successful, it doesn't necessarily mean that her process ends there. Rather, if she's smart, she'll continually look for new recipes and ways to improve her product; time-saving methods and systems; cost efficiencies, and the like.

The Four Most Critical Marketing Inputs

There are four essential inputs required for excellent marketing, which when combined with your actions, can literally make, or break, your business. They are:

1. *Mindset*: Your philosophies, attitudes, and beliefs.
2. *Assets*: Your resources—time, money, people, machines, systems.
3. *Skills*: Your talents—financial, managerial, technical, etc.
4. *Knowledge*: Your facts and figures—information on your company, competitors, marketplace, industry, customers, prospects, products, and services, etc.

Marketing Plan Outline

I. Executive Summary

A. Purpose: How this plan will be used

B. Introduction and overview

1. Company
2. Employees
3. Location
4. Service Area
5. Product and Service Offerings
6. 12-Month Business Objectives

C. Core Philosophies

1. Beliefs
2. Vision
3. Mission

D. Summary of Plan Objectives and Recommendations

1. Strategic Goals

2. Tactical Objectives

II. Situational Analysis (Strengths, Weaknesses, Opportunities, and Threats)

A. Company
B. Customers
C. Competitors
D. Climate
E. Collaborators

III. Marketing Strategies

A. Overall Strategy
B. Products and Services
C. Pricing
D. Target Markets and Segmentation
E. Positioning
F. Value Proposition and USP
G. Marketplace Message

IV. Tactics and Market Communication

A. Current Marketing Materials
B. Advertising
C. Programs, Promotions
D. Public Relations
E. Internet Marketing
F. Direct Sales
G. Activities List with Timelines and Task Owners

V. Budgets and Measurement

A. Marketing Budget
B. Measurements
C. Tools
D. Resources

Source: *The Procrastinator's Guide to Marketing (Or: How to Get Off Your Butt and Develop Your Marketing Plan!)* by Mary Eule Scarborough and David A. Scarborough (Entrepreneur Media, Inc., 2008)

MARKETING TIPS

The SWOT Analysis

SWOT (Strengths, Weaknesses, Opportunities, and Threats) is commonly used in business as a method of analyzing your ability to compete against other businesses that sell products or services similar to yours in the same marketplace and to the same target audience. Additionally, conducting a SWOT analysis can help you identify your position within the marketplace—how consumers view your business and products or services in direct relationship to your competition and their products or services. The true purpose of this book is to boil down business mumbo jumbo into easily digestible information bites that make sense and can be readily applied by small-business owners and managers. So, I have taken the "scratch your head factor" out of trying to make heads or tails of a SWOT analysis and broken it down into five simple steps.

Step 1. Definition

The first step is to simply understand what the strengths, weaknesses, opportunities, and threats are and how they relate to your particular business.

Strengths

Strengths are resources your business has that can be used as an advantage in business, or a specialty at which your business excels can be effectively used to reach your business and marketing objectives. For instance, a company strength might be that you have the most highly trained service technicians in your geographical trading area.

Weaknesses

Weakness is a critical factor that diminishes a company's competitiveness, a limitation that stands between you and your business and marketing objectives. An example of a weakness may be that your business lacks sufficient venture capital that could be used to stimulate growth.

Opportunities

An opportunity is best characterized as a positive situation upon which you can capitalize. A true opportunity can potentially improve your company's position in the marketplace and profitability. For instance, the recent deregulation of automated teller machines in Canada created opportunities for entrepreneurs to own banking machines and offer cash withdrawal and deposit services to consumers for a fee.

Threats

A threat is best characterized as a negative situation that can potentially damage your position in the marketplace and your profitability. For instance, the ATM example above represents a threat to the Canadian banking industry that once held a monopoly on the ownership and operation of ATMs. This threat came in the form of deregulation of the industry by the government to open the industry to enable private ATM ownership. The banks no longer control a monopoly and now face competition from the private business sector.

Step 2. Internal Analysis

The second step is to analyze the strengths and weaknesses within your business. This is best accomplished by using a blackboard, whiteboard, or large sheet of paper and later transferring the information to your computer to create and print the analysis.

Internal Strengths

Take a moment to consider what your company's strengths are and write them down. I always try to develop the list to include five strengths, but list only what I believe to be major strengths that are highly marketable. To develop your strengths list, ask yourself questions:

- What are your current competitive advantages in the marketplace?
- In what does your business specialize?
- What is the biggest benefit that people receive from buying your products or service?

The questions that you ask and your answers will be directly related to your business and what you sell. When you develop your questions and subsequently answer them, try to view the questions from your customer's perspective. Doing so may help you identify a new strength, or alternately reveal a weakness that you thought of as a strength.

Internal Weaknesses

Next, take a moment to consider what internal weaknesses your business has. Remember, weaknesses can come in any and all forms: poorly trained or motivated employees, cash flow problems, lack of credibility, or narrow product selection are just a few. Once again, write these down and try to include at least five major weak points that may diminish your ability to effectively compete in the marketplace. The questions you develop should be relative to your business and what you do or sell. Questions should revolve around important topics and issues:

- What are the causes of the current complaints we receive?
- What could we be doing better?
- What are we doing that is hurting our business?

Step 3. External Analysis

The third step is to analyze the external opportunities and threats that face your business. Once again, use a blackboard, whiteboard, or large sheet of paper and later transfer the information to your computer to create and print the analysis.

External Opportunities

Take a moment to consider what external opportunities may be currently available or coming available that could be capitalized upon for the benefit of your business. Here are some examples of external opportunities:

- Changes in technologies that would enable you to increase productivity or market share.
- Changing trends in consumer buying habits that would favor your product or service.
- Changing demographics in your trading area that would favor your particular business.
- Forthcoming changes in government rules and regulations on a local, state, or federal level that would have a positive impact on your business.

External opportunities can come in almost any form; for instance, the closing of one of your main competitors is an opportunity. Dig deep and try to identify at least five current or forthcoming external opportunities that could potentially benefit your business and prioritize them from the greatest opportunity to the least beneficial opportunity.

External Threats

Next, take a moment to consider what external threats your business might currently be facing or could face in the future and write them down. Here are some examples of external threats:

- Is there new or increased competition in the marketplace?
- Is your industry in the maturing or declining phase?
- Are there changes coming in government regulations or changing technologies that could have a negative impact on your business?

Step 4. Data Analysis

The fourth step is to carefully analyze and prioritize the data for each section. Start with strengths and list them from your greatest to your smallest. Repeat this for each of the internal and external categories. Often you will see patterns start to form, such as competitor strength built upon one of your internal weaknesses and so forth.

Step 5. SWOT Action Plan

Once you have analyzed and prioritized all of your data, you will be able to create an action plan covering the following.

Maximize Strengths

Knowing what your greatest internal strengths are will allow you to build upon them and maximize their positive impact on your business. For instance, if your great strength is your highly trained work force, then this should become your main competitive advantage and the cornerstone or anchor message for all your marketing activities.

Minimize Weaknesses

Knowing what your internal weaknesses are forces you to resolve them or work out ways to minimize their impact on your business. Often a SWOT analysis will work as an important "wake-up call to the facts" that no longer allows you to simply hope problems will go away.

Capitalize on Opportunities

Identifying external opportunities enables you to properly plan for the future. It also allows you to take immediate action and capitalize on opportunities that can have a positive impact on your business almost instantly.

Eliminate Threats

Now that you have identified external threats and how these can potentially affect your business and profitability, you can create a course of action that will reduce or entirely eliminate these threats. Or you may choose to simply find a way to avoid the threats if it is possible to do so without potential damage to your business.

Source: *Entrepreneur Magazine's Ultimate Small Business Marketing Guide* by James Stephenson with Courtney Thurman (Entrepreneur Press, 2007)

PROSPECTING

There are a multitude of reasons why you should always continue to prospect for new business, regardless of how busy your sales schedule might presently be, or how rosy your sales future looks. One of the most important reasons is that continual and systematic prospecting will ensure that your business pipeline remains full. Your pipeline consists of the prospects you are currently working with to turn their interest into sales. Take your core group of friends in high school or college and add up how many of those people you are still in contact with daily, weekly, or even yearly. If you're like most people, I'll bet you're in contact with less than 25 percent of them. The same thing happens to customers, they move, get lured to competitors, die, or their buying habits change. Where have my customers gone? This is one of the largest complaints of business owners and salespeople. After years in business or in selling, sales and profits begin to slide and a once loyal customer base is slowly vanishing—just like the group of friends from your school days. This is why it is important to continually prospect so that you can continually refill your pipeline with new contacts, prospects, and customers to whom you can sell and with whom you can do business.

Prospecting Basics

Ninety-five percent of what you have to say, the actions you have taken to get to this point in the sales cycle, or information related to and about your company is, for the most part, irrelevant to your prospect. They only want and need to know the remaining 5 percent, which when boiled down are the following three basic things.

The Basic Information

Your product or service and how you market it must be clear and easy to understand in moments, not hours or days. Consequently you must develop your sales message around clarity in order to appeal to the largest segment of your target audience. Make it plain English, easy to understand, and free of boring technical jargon that fits in great with scientific reports, but only works to confuse the vast majority of people. Never make what you do and why you do it hard for people to understand just for the benefit of your ego or to feel that it gives you a superior edge, because it doesn't. Sell more and profit by making your sales message clear and keeping your overall approach to sales and marketing simple and straightforward.

Benefit

What you sell has to benefit the person to whom you are trying to sell it. Living in balmy Vancouver, I have little use for a snowmobile no matter how many features it has and how much horsepower is stashed under the hood—but a rain jacket? Yes, that would be beneficial. Appeal to your target audience by giving them what they need, helping them fix a problem, making them rich, saving them money, or making them feel better. Selling is all about matching what you have to sell to what people need. Once again, if I need an umbrella and you're selling umbrellas, then your job of persuading me to buy one becomes rather easy, wouldn't you agree?

Value

What you sell has to represent value to your prospect. This means that regardless of the price, they see and can justify a direct correlation between your offering and the price that goes with it, and what that offering will do for them—fill a need, solve a problem, or whatever it may be. Products and services are only worth what people will pay for them, but the more value (benefits) that a person can derive from a product or service, the more they are likely to pay for it.

Qualifying: Needs

Qualify your prospect's needs is perhaps the most overused advice featured in a multitude of marketing books, but very sound and timeless advice just the same. The first rule of qualifying is to determine if the prospect needs what you are selling. If not, you are wasting your time and theirs by continuing with the conversation. If you have an in-depth knowledge of what you sell and how it will benefit buyers then qualifying a prospect in terms of needs should be easily accomplished with a few simple questions. What problems need solving? What are their requirements? What needs to be improved? What is wrong with what they currently have, or, alternatively, what would make their job or life easier? Of course, there is one exception to the "qualifying needs rule," which is appeal to emotions in such a way that it overrides and sometimes defies logic. Good examples of this is the fact that few people need a hot tub, but many want one, and few people actually need a Rolex wristwatch, but once again many want them. However, even with that said, unless you are selling a product or service that can be sold strictly on an emotional level wherein for the most part logic can be thrown out the window, stick with the time-tested and proven qualifying concept of only pursuing prospects who truly need what you are selling, regardless of how tempting the challenge might be to try to close them. Always ask yourself what is the best use of your time at that very moment; I will guarantee it is not trying to sell something to someone who doesn't need or want it.

Qualifying: Decision-Maker

Take the time to ask and make sure that you are dealing with the person who can ultimately make the decision in terms of buying your products or services. And if the person you are dealing with is not the decision-maker then find out who is and deal with that person or group of people. Nothing is more frustrating than having a hot prospect on the line only to discover after spending much time and energy with him that he cannot make a decision about buying your product or service. Or, that there are other people who will be involved in the decision-making process besides this one person. The best way to find out who is the decision-maker to simply ask your prospect with questions such as: "Who will be making the purchasing decision? "Will you be making the decision on your own, or will there be other people involved in the purchasing decision?" "If you find my [product] suitable are you authorized to make the purchase?" However, take your prospect's response with a grain of salt because even if someone tells you that they will be personally making decisions in terms of buying, that is not always entirely the case. Lower and middle managers sometimes want to feel important, but ultimately they have to secure approvals from people higher up on the managing chain before they can give the go-ahead. You can get around this by asking your prospect a few times throughout the initial questions phase more qualifying questions to do with decision-making. Generally if they are not truly the decision-maker that will come out in the conversation through their responses to your qualifying questions.

Qualifying: Time Line

What is the prospect's buying time line? Meaning when does she want to buy a particular product or service? And, the second aspect of qualifying time line is how committed is your prospect to her buying schedule? Very committed, somewhat committed, or just tentative based on other factors that could influence the final buying decision? Reveal this by asking questions. You can learn more about a prospect's needs in terms of timing by asking easy open-ended questions such as: "How soon do you need the [product]?" "When will you be ready to have the product installed?" "What is your time frame for completing this project?" "When would you like to take delivery?" These are very non-threatening questions and the beauty of asking time line questions early on, when you first meet a prospect, is the fact that the answers she gives will also give you a good indication as to her openness to an early close in the sales cycle. Top sales professionals have discovered that if a prospect answers positively to a qualifying time line question then an early trial close is not out of question even if you have not completed the entire qualifying process. So if a prospect tells you she needs it next week, respond, "If I can arrange for delivery next week, are you prepared to make the purchase?"

Qualifying: Financial

Qualifying prospects financially is where many salespeople become unglued because they feel uncomfortable asking people questions about their personal or business financial situation. Add to this, even if you do ask the right questions, the answers you receive might be somewhat embellished simply due to the fact that everyone wants to be perceived as being better off financially than they are in reality.

So where does that leave you? It leaves you knowing two things for sure. The first is that you must get comfortable and in the habit of asking prospects qualifying questions about their abilities to pay for the product or service, or their abilities to secure credit to pay for the product or service. Ask your prospects if they have the money put aside to pay for the purchase, if they will be using credit cards or arranging financing, or if you can take the liberty of arranging financing for them. You have to know that your prospect can financially afford to pay, by whatever means, before you invest time, energy, and money in the sales process. Second, you have to be realistic in regard to your prospect's purchasing power. This is not to say that you should assume your prospects cannot afford what they want or that they are blowing you a little smoke—not at all. But you should be prepared with an alternative and less expensive option or choice should financial matters become an obstacle to the sale. If you spend all your time focused on one product or service and suddenly money becomes an issue, then you have little room to move. However, if you keep in mind the notion that money could become an issue or obstacle and have a plan in place should that happen then you will be armed to save the sale and still do business with your prospect.

Time Management for Prospecting Success

It stands to reason that the better you manage your time, the more time you will be able to devote to prospecting for new business. Here are a few tricks that you can employ to maximize and make the best use of your time so that you will be able to devote more time to prospecting and closing.

- Maximize your prospecting and selling time by using prospect and customer management automated software.
- Set aside a block of time each day strictly for the purposes of prospecting, creating new ways to promote your products or services, and unique ways to position what you sell in the marketplace.
- Prepare your daily to-do list the evening before and strive to check off every item before you call it quits the following day.
- Develop a scheduling system and stick to it. Prospect the same time each day when you are most likely to reach your target audience on the phone or in person. Group presentations together to save time and stay in the same focused mindset. And, do all administrative work at the same time, once again to save time and stay focused on an individual task. Basically, organize your time so that you group together activities such as prospecting, presentations, research, follow up, and administrative tasks.
- Never procrastinate—clear all inquiries, problems, and customer requests by the end of each day. Only carry over things that cannot be immediately accomplished or resolved because of situations beyond your immediate control or information, people, products, or services to which you do not have immediate access.
- Block off rest and relaxation time to pursue hobbies and family activities each week and strive not to forgo them or alter the time you assign for them.
- Carry a "hot prospects" folder with you so that you can benefit from any unexpected down time by calling them or working on solutions to fix their product or service problems or needs. Inspirational ideas are lost if they are not written down in an easily retrievable format.
- Keep your goals and objectives written down and in front of you as a daily motivator.

Thou Shalt Never Prejudge

Prospecting Rule number one: Thou shalt never prejudge prospects' abilities to buy and pay for purchases, or their motivation for their choices. We have all heard the tale of the person who goes into the car dealership dressed shabbily only to be treated poorly by the salesperson on the floor. The salesperson prejudged the prospect based on appearances and without asking a single question came to the conclusion that this person could not possibly afford to purchase a new car. The story goes on to reveal that the prospect later returned to the dealership asking to talk to the sales manager. He then produced a bag of cash and said that because of the way he was treated earlier by the salesperson he just thought the manager should know that his bag full of money would be spent at the competition, where he would be purchasing a new car. There are many versions of this story floating around—some may be based on fact and others fictional urban legends. Nevertheless the general premise is accurate—never prejudge prospects' abilities or motivation until careful questions and answers have established what they need, when they need it, if they can make the decision to buy, and if they have the financial ability to pay for it. Until these questions have been asked and answers given, everyone must be consider equally as a prospect regardless of looks, actions, dress, or speech.

Thou Shalt Never Express Personal Opinions

Prospecting rule number two: Thou shalt never initiate or be drawn into a political, religious, cultural, egotistical, or moral debate or discussion with any prospect or customer regardless of how strongly you may feel about the topic or subject matter. The best way not to offend a prospect or customer consciously or subconsciously is to simply avoid any controversial topics and issues. More than a few times I have sat through lectures, ramblings, and long-winded speeches given by prospects about what is wrong with everything under the sun and then some. Once I was even lectured by a university professor for close to an hour about why I should aspire to higher things in life than selling home renovations. (I was 28 years old at the time and earning in excess of five figures monthly and, more important, loved what I did.) Needless to say I bit my tongue a few times during his rant, smiled politely, and when I left I had a signed contract and a deposit check toward a $30,000 renovation project. The point is this: all people have a right to express their own opinions and take comfort in their own beliefs regardless of what those opinions and beliefs might be. But the job of a sales professional is not to debate issues or express opinions and thoughts on topics not related to the sale; it is to seek, qualify, close the sale, and ask for referrals, period.

Practice Immediate Follow-Up

All salespeople should get in the habit of immediately following up with new prospects after meetings to reconfirm what was discussed during the meeting and the course of action that will follow. You can do this in various ways: e-mail, fax, on the telephone, or by writing a letter and mailing it to them or having it delivered by courier. The benefits of immediate follow-up are many. First, it is an opportunity to compile all the information that was discussed at the meeting and to reconfirm the information, right down to the smallest detail. Second, it illustrates to prospects that you are interested in their needs, you want to solve their problems, and that you conduct business in a very professional manner. And third, practicing immediate follow-up provides you with a great opportunity to restate all of the details with your prospect so that there will be no miscommunications when you get back together for the sales presentation. Personally, I like to talk by telephone with the prospect and take notes; from that I write down everything from the first meeting and the follow-up telephone call, reconfirming all the details. Then I fax the notes to the prospect and often ask that she sign or initial the pages and fax them back.

Clone Your Best Customers

You know who your best customers are—they are the people who frequently buy products or services from you, always pay on time and in full, refer others to your business, and rarely complain. Now wouldn't it be nice if all of your customers were the same and you had thousands just like them? Well the thought might not be as big a pipe dream as you think. Industry-leading businesspeople take the time to identify who their best customers are, and then set out to clone them. This means they identify common characteristics of their best customers and develop marketing and action plans aimed at people who are similar to their best customers. Granted, few small businesses can afford to conduct such in-depth research and have these analysis plans created. However, every small-business owner can afford to create a simple questionnaire and politely ask their best customers to complete it. Questions should refer to their interest and hobbies, the type of publications they like to read, radio and television programs they like to listen to and watch, and basic questions pertaining to education, income, family, and career. You can use the response information to identify patterns, things your best customers have in common with each other. Perhaps a high percentage of them subscribe to the same newspaper; then it would be wise to advertise you business in that newspaper to appeal to people who are like your best customers. Or, maybe a high percentage belong to one or more community associations; logically then you would want to join those associations and network with the members. There is much wisdom to the old adage "birds of a feather flock together." Identify as many feathers that your best customers have in common as you can and you won't be far from discovering where the entire flock is located.

Source: *Entrepreneur Magazine's Ultimate Small Business Marketing Guide* by James Stephenson with Courtney Thurman (Entrepreneur Press, 2007)

THE 200 PERSUASIVE WORDS FOR MARKETING

A

Absolutely
Advice
Amazing
Announcing
Anticipation
Appeal
Appreciative
Approved
Attention
Attractive
Authentic

B

Bargain
Beautiful
Believe
Benefit
Best
Big
Blowout
Brand name
Bright
Budget
Buy

C

Call
Care
Challenge
Choose
Cost
Clearance
Compare
Complete
Confidential
Convenient

D

Delicious
Delivered
Dependable
Deserve
Development
Direct
Discount
Discover
Drastically

E

Easy
Endorsed
Event
Excellent
Exciting
Exclusive
Expert
Extra

Extravaganza

F

Fabulous
Fact
Family
Famous
Fantastic
Fascinating
Fast
Feel
Fortune
Free
Fresh
Full

G

Gain
Genuine
Get
Gift
Gigantic
Give
Go
Great
Guarantee

H

Have
Health
Hello
Help
Helpful
Highest
Honest
Huge
Hurry

I

Important
Improve
Incredible
Informative
Interesting
Introducing
Invited

K

Keep
Knowledge

L

Largest
Latest
Learn
Lifetime
Limited
Look
Love
Low

M

Magic
Miracle
Modern
More
Most

N

Need

New
News
Now

O
Offer
Official
Open
Opportunity
Outstanding

P
Personalized
Please
Popular
Powerful
Practical
Present
Price
Professional
Profitable
Promise
Protect
Proud
Proven

Q
Qualified
Quality
Quick

R
Rate
Ready
Real
Reassurance
Recommended
Redeemable
Reduced
Referred
Refundable
Relax
Reliable
Remarkable
Responsible
Reputation
Results
Revolutionary
Reward
Rich
Right
Rush

S
Safety
Satisfaction
Save
Secret
Secure
Security
Selected
Selection
Self-confidence
Sensational
Service
Simple
Smart
Smile
Special

Start
Startling
Strong
Sturdy
Successful
Suddenly
Superior
Support
Surprise

T

Take care
Team
Terrific
Tested
Thank you
Time
Today
Tremendous
Trust
Try

U

Ultimate
Unconditional
Understand
Unique
Unlimited
Useful

V

Valuable
Vast

W

Want
Wanted
Warranty
Wealth
Welcome
Win
Wise
Wonderful

Y

Yes
You
Youthful

Source: *Entrepreneur Magazine's Ultimate Small Business Marketing Guide* by James Stephenson with Courtney Thurman (Entrepreneur Press, 2007)

15 FOOLPROOF IDEAS FOR PROMOTING YOUR COMPANY

Every successful company uses some sort of promotion to influence certain audiences—usually customers or prospects—by informing or persuading them. Reasons for promoting a business include: increasing visibility, adding credibility to you or your company, enhancing or improving your image, and bringing in new business. The following cost-effective, easy-to-execute ideas have the power to increase sales in a way conventional advertising cannot. The key is to find the methods that are appropriate for your clients' business, marketplace, and professional style.

1. *Contests.* As one example, a cookware store decided to sponsor cooking contests. After sending out a press release announcing a competition for the best cookie or chocolate cake, a mailing went to the store's customers soliciting entries. Food editors, professional chefs, and cooking teachers were invited to be judges. Both the winners and their winning recipes were publicized. Essay and design contests are also possibilities, such as a furniture store establishing a prize for student furniture design. Pie eating, pancake flipping, oyster shucking, and grape stomping contests make sense for restaurants. Dentists can hold smile contests, video rental stores can stage movie trivia quizzes.
2. *Newsletters.* Another good way to promote, particularly for brokers, banks, and business consultants, is through newsletters. They demonstrate how much you know about your field and do it in a low-key, informative way. They help keep your company high in the consciousness of your prospects.
3. *Demonstrations.* Demonstrations are a way to attract people to your place of business, show them how to best use your product, and establish your credibility. A retail/wholesale fish outlet holds cooking demonstrations twice a week, featuring a different restaurant chef each time and attracting substantial crowds. Recipe cards are even given out. Wallpaper demonstrations, fashion shows, gift wrapping, refinishing, and computer demonstrations have all worked well for retailers selling products associated with them.
4. *Seminars.* Often more appropriate for business-to-business marketing, seminars are the commercial side of demonstrations. If you hold a seminar, follow these rules for success: Schedule the event at a time convenient to most attendees; be specific in the invitation about when the event begins, and ends, who will be there, and what the agenda is; follow up the invitations with personal phone calls; charge for the seminar to give it a higher perceived value; follow up after the event to get people's reactions.

5. *Premiums.* Also called an advertising specialty, a premium is a gift of some kind that reminds your customer of you and your service. There are thousands from which to choose: key chains, coffee mugs, refrigerator magnets, baseball caps, paperweights—just about anything that can be engraved, imprinted, silk-screened, or embroidered with your company name, phone number, and website.
6. *Speeches.* Depending on your topic and market, you might want to speak before Chambers of Commerce, trade associations, parent groups, senior citizens, or other local organizations.
7. *Articles.* Another possibility is to write an article for a trade journal, reprint it, and mail it off to your friends, customers, and prospects. This positions you as an expert, and is a particularly good way to promote a consulting business.
8. *Bonuses.* If you have a restaurant, give away a glass of wine with dinner to introduce a new menu. If you sell to retailers, give them a display fixture with the order of a gross. If you sell office supplies, give away a new pen with a sizeable purchase. If you're in the cosmetics business, offer customers a free sample blusher when they buy mascara and lipstick.
9. *Coupons.* For best results, the price break should be significant—at least 15 percent. This is one of the least expensive ways to develop new trade and an excellent tool for evaluating advertising. However, one theory holds that coupons draw people who only buy discount and never become regular customers, so be sure to monitor the results.
10. *Donations.* Donating your product or service to a charitable cause often results in positive exposure to community leaders, charity board members, PTAs, and civic groups. While consumer products are most desired, many organizations also look for donations of professional service time. If you have a restaurant or a large meeting facility, consider hosting an event for a charitable organization. This works best if volunteers for that charity are potential customers.
11. *Samples.* No matter what you do to promote your business, giving potential customers a sample is an excellent way to attract attention and make a positive impression. In many cases, it makes just as much sense to spend your marketing and advertising dollars on giving out your own products as buying advertisements, especially if cash is tight. The key is to give samples to the audience you want to reach, i.e., software packages to computer user groups or nutritious snacks to health-oriented consumers. In the food arena, where one taste is worth a thousand words, firms now exist that test-market new products for large and small companies alike through in-store demonstrations. A good demonstration company not only keeps track of how much of your product was given away, but also submits detailed reports on what people said about the product and how much of it was purchased.

12. *Free Trials.* If your product is too big or expensive to give away outright, why not offer a free trial to qualified customers? Try shipping it to prospects with no strings attached. Most people will appreciate the opportunity to try the product, and hopefully many will like it enough to buy it.
13. *Free Services.* If you can't afford to give away products, offering your services as a way of generating new business can also pay off. For example, if you own a retail clothing business, send out a flyer offering customers a free fashion consultation to draw them into the store.
14. *Special Benefits, Rates, or Notices.* Smart organizations go out of their way to make customers feel important and appreciated. Frequent flyer clubs are the most pervasive example of loyalty-building benefits for customers only. This method has been adapted by many kinds of businesses. Most software companies sell program updates to customers at discounted prices, and advance notices about sales, changes, or opportunities can help cement customer ties.
15. *Say Thanks.* One of the best ways to let customers know you value their business and encourage their continued patronage is also one of the easiest. It boils down to saying thank you in letters, mailers, surveys, statement stuffers, receipts, invoices, and in person.

Source: U.S. Small Business Administration

NETWORKING AND REFERRAL CHECKLIST

Evaluate your networking and referral skills by using this checklist. If you answer No to any question, consider how you can incorporate that activity into your operation.

Yes	No	
❑	❑	Do you set networking and referrals objectives and goals, and use these objectives and goals to measure your success?
❑	❑	Do you carry a file in your car stocked with a good supply of marketing brochures, business cards, and promotional items for handouts at meetings and functions?
❑	❑	Do you have and maintain an up-to-date prospect and customer contact database?
❑	❑	Do you follow up immediately with all new networking contacts you make?
❑	❑	Are you one of the first people to arrive and one of the last to leave networking meetings and functions?
❑	❑	Do you always exchange business cards when you meet someone and write notes on the back of the card you receive that better describe the person's business?
❑	❑	Do you provide special incentives and gifts in exchange for referrals?
❑	❑	Do you make a point of tapping suppliers and business alliances for referrals?
❑	❑	Do you freely offer business owners you meet referrals with no strings attached?
❑	❑	Do you keep the lines of communication open with past clients and try to develop strategies to lure them back as customers?
❑	❑	Before attending an event or meeting do you get names of people and companies that will be participating and conduct basic research so that you know something about them?

Yes	No	
❑	❑	Do you carefully track your referral sources and dedicate more networking time where it will have the greatest impact on your business?
❑	❑	Do you try to set up meetings right away with people you meet rather than telling them you will call, or they can call you?
❑	❑	Do you promptly follow up on all referrals you receive, at least within 48 hours?
❑	❑	Do you have the current membership lists for all of the clubs, groups, and associations to which you belong, business and social?
❑	❑	Do you strive to know other people's businesses better so that you can secure better qualified leads for them?
❑	❑	Do you swap customer and lead lists with other businesspeople in your community?
❑	❑	Do you write columns and articles in your field of expertise and seek out opportunities to get them published in print and electronic media?
❑	❑	Do you mine newspapers and magazines for new selling and business opportunities?
❑	❑	Do you offer free reports, conduct training workshops, speak at seminars, and teach in your field of expertise, and share as much of your expert knowledge as possible?
❑	❑	Do you know your customers' and business contacts' special dates, such as birthdays and anniversaries, and do you always send a card or gift on these dates?
❑	❑	Do you keep in close personal contact with all current customers, at least once a month?
❑	❑	Do you commit to attending at least one function a week where there may be networking opportunities available?
❑	❑	Do you regularly attend trade shows and seminars to form new business alliances and make new contacts?
❑	❑	Do you sit beside people you have not met before and introduce yourself to new members at meetings you attend?

Yes	No	
❑	❑	Do you often host brainstorming meetings and sessions with employees, suppliers, and business alliances to seek input and advice in terms of marketing activities and ways to generate new business?
❑	❑	Have you created a memorable personal trademark so that you stand out at meetings and events?
❑	❑	Have you developed a mini sales pitch that is short, powerful, memorable, and clearly states the biggest benefit of what you do or sell?
❑	❑	Are you known as a credible and reliable source of information at the meetings you attend?
❑	❑	Can you clearly explain the products or services you sell in less than 30 seconds?
❑	❑	Do you know your competition inside out and upside down, but never slander them in any way, shape, or form?
❑	❑	Do you listen more than you talk when you meet new people?
❑	❑	Do you keep abreast of current events so that you can carry on meaningful conversations?
❑	❑	Do you freely share great marketing ideas with people you meet?
❑	❑	Do you always take time out to make introductions and network in the vicinity of your current projects and jobs in progress?
❑	❑	Do you go out of your way to get involved in community groups, associations, clubs, and events?
❑	❑	Have you joined business groups such as the chamber of commerce and specific business networking groups in your area?
❑	❑	Do you go out of your way to welcome newcomers to the area and freely give them helpful advice about their new community?
❑	❑	Have you created and do you use a bold nametag? And have you developed memorable introductions that clearly state the biggest customer benefit of what you do or what you sell?
❑	❑	Do you continually measure the effectiveness of your networking activities?

Yes	No	
❑	❑	Do you have the attitude of a host at meetings and events as opposed to the attitude of a guest?
❑	❑	Do you always try to say yes when asked to speak publicly?
❑	❑	Have you made memorable donations such as imprinted coffee mugs or a wall clock to your networking group?
❑	❑	Do you go online to network for new business and participate in online discussion groups and forums?
❑	❑	Do you hold an annual contest or sweepstake of some sort to collect leads for follow-up and qualifying?

Source: *Entrepreneur Magazine's Ultimate Small Business Marketing Guide* by James Stephenson with Courtney Thurman (Entrepreneur Press, 2007)

Appendix B
Crisis Management Lessons Learned

Crisis management is an important aspect of public relations. Crisis management expert Jonathan Bernstein offers these 50 lessons learned from various situations with which he has helped his clients over the years. They are not prioritized in any way because what was the most important lesson for one person or firm might not be for another. He notes that many of the lessons relate to internet-centered activity, so be sure your clients have an internet crisis management strategy and capabilities.

1. One hostile and/or ego-driven person with a computer and some internet savvy can do a huge amount of damage to any organization.

2. Damaging information present on the internet spreads virally, being reprinted by other websites or even news organizations regardless of accuracy. Ignoring it will only make matters worse.

3. All legal threats—e.g. threatened lawsuits, regulatory investigations—are potential threats to reputation and should be brought to the attention of whoever is responsible for reputation management/PR as soon as they're identified. Typically,

however, legal counsel and even senior company management delay notifying their PR advisor, internal or external, until the stuff hits the fan or is about to, imminently. Rushed consideration of PR strategy and messaging is seldom as good as that which can be produced given more lead time.

4. There are PR agencies and consultants who do not think about or, out of greed or ego, fail to consider how much damage they do to their clients by claiming to have more crisis management capabilities than, in fact, they do.
5. Mid- to large-size organizations, in particular, need an automated system of notifying their crisis-management-related teams and impacted stakeholders instantly and concurrently. Relying on human "call chains" by people who have other responsibilities and/or who are also trying to put out the fire is unrealistic and results in delay and more damage.
6. Sometimes it's wiser to make peace than be right.
7. Even organizations who think they are transparent in their internal communications are usually surprised to learn about some of the flaws uncovered by a vulnerability audit.
8. The ability to make a flawless personal presentation to 1,000 people at a conference does not automatically translate, without training, to an ability to conduct an on-camera media interview related to a crisis.
9. Don't get into a public spat with government agencies or the media, they carry bigger sticks than you do and have long memories.
10. With rare exception, media interview skills were not part of a CEO's scholastic experience and—even if they were—they have eroded to the point of uselessness if not practiced.
11. Any significant operational decision has a public relations impact, internally or externally, and should be considered in that light before being finalized. Some decisions, which seem to make perfect sense financially, for example, may end up seriously damaging relationships with stakeholders and, ultimately, cost money versus saving it.
12. Everyone in your organization, from highest-paid tolowest, should understand what your organization considers to be a crisis.
13. Everyone in your organization, from highest-paid to lowest, should understand what their individual responsibilities are for crisis response.

14. The actions of every employee and contractors considered, *de facto*, to be part of your organization have the impact to promote or damage your reputation.

15. Be very, very careful about what you say or don't say in email! Anything put into email can be (a) leaked; (b) inadvertently distributed to the wrong people; (c) legally damaging; and (d) revealed through the disclosure process in any formal legal proceeding.

16. With regard to media interviews, if you don't say it, they can't use it. It is rare (although not completely unheard of) for a reporter to actually make up a quote. When spokespersons claim that this has happened, usually it's because they have been sucked in to a leading question, e.g., reporter: "Mr. Smith, do you think that this is the worst thing that has ever happened to your company." Smith: "Yeah, maybe." Sentence that appears in the paper: "This may be the worst thing that has ever happened to our company," said Smith.

17. It's much wiser to encourage and even reward internal whistle-blowing than to find yourself at the wrong end of news coverage, a lawsuit, and/or a governmental investigation prompted by a whistle-blower.

18. The court of public opinion can destroy your organization much more quickly than a court of law.

19. Criticism is only damaging if your stakeholders believe it—but never assume you know, without asking, what your stakeholders believe!

20. Crisis communications and emergency response plans are not created to provide a flawless method of response to every crisis situation. They are created to establish a system for effective response to any crisis and to serve as a basis for training crisis responders.

21. If you think a crisis-related response mechanism will work, but you've never tested and trained with it, you're inviting much higher levels of damage when the crisis occurs.

22. More and more attorneys general initiate their investigations based on stories written and/or produced by consumer reporters. The corollary: If you directly serve consumers, consumer reporters are a special risk for which you must plan, because they will respond to inaccurate allegations as if they were the truth and do not like to produce headlines that read, "Consumer Allegation Proven False by Responsible Company."

23. Companies that respond well to crises can actually gain market share and enhance their reputation.

24. If crisis preparedness does not receive the full support of an organization's leadership—particularly the CEO—the organization will not be prepared, even if they have some plans on the shelf and a bit of training to go with it.

25. No person or organization has a reputation so fine that they are immune to reputation threats from within or without. The arrogance inherent in denying this reality has been a major contributing factor to innumerable crises.

26. We have probably not seen the end of food- and product-related crises originating in the People's Republic of China. Any organization with relevant connections to the PRC should factor this into their crisis preparedness.

27. The internet continues to make it easy to read about, hear, and view skeletons in your closet. Corollary lesson: Conduct your business as if everything you write, say, and do might be recorded and you'll avoid a lot of crises (P.S. There will be 300 million multimedia-capable mobile phones shipped in 2008).

28. Intra-organizational infighting is one of the leading causes of crises and plays a major role in exacerbating crises that may otherwise have remained minor.

29. No written statement can transmit crisis-related messages as well as video communication.

30. If you're a technophobic CEO, get the heck out of the way and let your techno-savvy staff and/or consultants guide you on the best ways to use technology for crisis management purposes.

31. The Better Business Bureau (at least in the United States) can be a royal pain in the ass to deal with because of its institutionalized bias and bad habit of presenting information out of context. Unfortunately it's probably still worth your reputation management time to be highly responsive to BBB complaints and to be a member as well. BBB complaints are often cited by your critics and it's a very common destination for consumers deciding whether to do business with you.

32. Ignore a committed online critic and he'll take most of the top Google rankings under your preferred search terms.

33. The most predictable judge or jury is unpredictable. Always prepare for multiple potential outcomes in litigation-related crisis management.

34. Every organization in the world needs a blog.

35. Changing copy less than once per week on a blog created as a primary communications vehicle (versus strictly for SEO purposes) is like riding a horse in the middle of the German Autobahn—everyone's going to pass you by or run you down. If you don't know what "SEO" means, see lesson #30, above.

36. Too many organizations engage in Search Engine Obfuscation instead of Search Engine Optimization, enhancing their vulnerability to crises.

37. Policies vital to avoiding and/or minimizing the damage from crises must be accompanied by initial and refresher training or they are worthless. Corollary lesson: Almost every functional area of an organization has (or should have!) such policies.

38. When there are significant cultural differences between the foreign owners of a company and the natives of the country in which they're doing business, those owners must be willing to defer crisis communications strategy and decisions to those who best understand the culture(s) in which they are communicating.

39. If organizational leaders make a commitment to their stakeholders, they should make certain that everyone in their organization (a) is aware of the commitment and (b) does nothing to violate it, or the entire organization's credibility can suffer immense and completely preventable damage.

40. Few organizations have telephone systems or website servers capable of managing the dramatic increase in traffic that would result from a crisis. And many of those who think they do haven't tested their systems through simulation exercises.

41. If I emptied ten trashcans in the executive suite (and many other parts) of most organizations at the end of a workday, I would find information that could compromise the reputation and/or financial well-being and/or security of those organizations.

42. If you are likely to need certain types of products or services as a result of the types of crises most common to an organization such as yours (e.g., backup generators, testing laboratories), the time to establish relationships with product/service providers is now, not under the gun of a crisis. Corollary lesson: During times of widespread crises, such as a natural disaster, demand for certain types of products/services is higher than the supply; "preferred customers" move to the front of the line, last-minute customers may not be served at all.

43. It's a mistake to let crisis response depend on the leadership skills of any single individual, no matter how talented and charismatic he/she might be. Crisis

response should be based on advanced planning that generates a system for effective response, which works even when individual team members are unavailable at the time the crisis occurs.

44. PR representatives for any organization need to be very familiar not only with traditional media, but with leading bloggers covering their industry. In times of crisis, leading bloggers can become more important than traditional media: they are more prolific, more focused on a subject over the long-term, and more frequently quoted by other bloggers.

45. Not all IT departments or consultants are created equal. Some think they understand all the ways in which the information on their systems can be compromised—some of them are wrong.

46. Far too many organizations have no contingency plan whatsoever for what to do if—tonight—they permanently or long term lost access to their primary workplace or a major facility due to a disaster of kind (e.g., fire, flood, earthquake, tornado, hurricane).

47. There are relatively few organizations that have functional disaster response plans—functional meaning that they include all details of what to do in the event of a man-made or natural disaster and that training has accompanied the plans, including drills and/or exercises.

48. Many crises, from reputational threats to threats of violence, have been foreshadowed by messages on traditional websites, blogs, or social media sites, but most organizations fail to regularly monitor these online locations. Those seeking to harm individuals or an organization have the portable ability to easily record the written word, audio, and video, and post it on the internet very quickly—or even live.

49. Quite a few organizations have a policy of not allowing their top leaders to fly together, yet they are actually at more risk driving together, which they do all the time.

50. While many organizations go to great length to protect the security of data stored on their servers, the same organizations usually allow executives (and others) to have notebook computers on which they store sensitive information. Those notebook computers, which are taken to public places and are highly vulnerable to theft, are seldom secured by anything more than a password, which is easily bypassed.

Source: Jonathan Bernstein, Bernstein Crisis Management, bernsteincrisismanagement.com

Appendix C
Search Engine Optimization Ethics and Guidelines

A discussion of search engine optimization (SEO) would not be complete without addressing what happens when good SEO goes bad. As with other things, many of the practices that are frowned on were once legitimate. However, when good practices are overused or used for bad purposes, it penalizes everyone.

SEO, like every other discipline, has those who follow legitimate, industry-accepted practices and those who strive to "trick" the system with dirty tricks. Industry insiders refer to unethical or unfair practices as "black hat SEO."

The terms "white hat" and "black hat" were actually taken from old cowboy movies. In these movies the good guy always wore a white hat and the bad guy always wore a black hat. So the sheriff of the town would ride in with a white hat to fight off the robbers who wore black hats. For ages in Western history, black has often been associated with darkness, shadows, and evil, and white has stood as a symbol of goodness and purity.

In the cyberworld, the term "black hat" was first used in reference to hacking, but the basic principles are the same when it comes to SEO.

However, there's debate about what is "unfair or unethical." A common thread to what is black hat is "unfair manipulation." Some would argue that SEO in and of itself is a manipulative tactic. After all, the purpose of SEO is to manipulate the search engines into ranking your site higher, right? Wrong! SEO and SEM (search engine marketing) are equivalent to creating advertising messages for television, magazines, or other format. You strive to gain the attention of your target audience—the audience that needs and desires what you sell. You aren't trying to twist their arms and falsely manipulate them into buying your product or service.

This false assumption about sales and marketing is why so many fail at the practices. If you believe that selling is mind manipulation, you may trick a few people into buying your goods and services, but you won't create long-term, sustainable relationships. My goal is to share with you good, sound practices and the underlying principles that will help you earn money not only today but also well into the future. I believe good business is based on relationship, and a foundation built on deceit and trickery does not support that goal.

What is considered black hat SEO varies. Sometimes black hat is designated by search engine guidelines. The practice itself may not be unethical but simply scowled on by the search engine. There are black hat practices that intentionally set out to harm the competition. These tactics are widely embraced as wrong. Black hat sometimes involves property rights (stealing content from others). The biggest debates about black hat are practices so designated because they result in "unnatural rankings." It's important to understand the many facets of SEO so that you'll know what not to do. Some practices that may appear harmless can get you in trouble with search engines. I believe that if you aren't hurting anyone, you're following the best rule. For example, if a mother searches for a baby stroller and is taken to an adult site instead, that could be considered "hurting" another person. Don't do that.

Webmasters who use white hat SEO techniques are as concerned about their visitors' experience on their websites as they are with ranking high on search engines. Thus, they concentrate on creating content that both their visitors and search engines are hungry for, forming legitimate relationships with other websites for link building, and proper use of meta tags.

What You Should Not Do: Black Hat SEO

So let's talk about black hat SEO. Black hat SEO optimization has no consideration for website visitors. Its only goal is to get ranked high in search engines. Black hat SEO optimization techniques are considered "spamdexing."

Spamdexing (content spam, link spam, and cloaking are examples) is a practice that tries to manipulate the search engines' indexing to produce higher ranking results. An example of spamdexing is *keyword stuffing*. In keyword stuffing, you stuff your web pages with competitive keywords simply to manipulate search engines rather than deliver useful content to the user. The content may not even make sense. It's simply a trick to manipulate the engines to rank you higher. You can also "overstuff" the page's meta tags.

Duplicate Content

As Google defines it, duplicate content means you have the exact same text on a different page in the same site. This also applies to sister sites or sites to which you are heavily linked. Avoiding duplicate content doesn't mean that every single word on all of your pages must be unique. Black hat duplication is copying and pasting the same paragraphs from one page to another. This practice can, and most likely will, drop your site's rankings and possibly exclude content from the main index. Syndicated content is not treated as duplicate content, so if you carry a news feed on your homepage that may also be found on 1,000 other websites, the search engines won't drop your ranking for it.

Note that syndicate content (distribution of pages/content via syndicated networks) is highly contested in terms of how much it can affect your site in the rankings, and it is a much-discussed topic on the search forums and at search conferences. Suggestions about "freshness" of data and origins are still being offered.

Link farming is the process of exchanging reciprocal links with websites to increase SEO. The idea behind link farming is to increase the number of sites that link to yours, because search engines such as Google rank sites according to, among other things, the quality and quantity of sites that link to them. In theory, the more sites that link to yours, the higher your ranking in the search engine results because more links indicate a higher level of popularity among internet users. However, search engines such as Google consider link farming to be a form of spam and have implemented procedures to banish sites that participate in link farming, so it has garnered negative connotations across the internet.

The difference between good link building and bad link building is in how it's done. Link spamming is another type of link farming in which you use software to generate lots of links over a short time. Google in particular looks unfavorably at lots of links created over a short time, and not naturally, with varying anchor text changes. Google refrains from the use of the term "reciprocal link exchanges" in its documentation.

There are many service providers who promise to help you boost your link popularity by automatically entering you into link exchange programs they operate. The programs often link your page to websites that have nothing to do with your content. Users should be aware of the repercussions of this action, as the major search engines penalize sites that participate in link farming, thereby negating the intended effect. A link farm is a web page that's nothing more than a page of links to other sites.

As I said earlier, some practices are black hat because the search engine frowns on the practice. For this reason, it's important to read the webmaster guidelines provided by the search engines. Google, in particular, may punish you by banishing your site to the still-existing supplemental index (fondly known as Google Hell) and you may not even understand why or how you got there!

That's why you must understand the good and bad so you'll know what not to do.

Google's supplemental index is like the digital basement. You're still listed on Google, but not in the more visible core index. Relegation to the supplemental index can significantly impact your revenues. A few things that can relegate you to the basement are duplicate content, a lack of links to other quality sites (yes, confusing, you can't have too few or too many), and pages with only a few words and pictures and little content.

Office politics have made their way to cyberspace, as well. Black hat sabotage is unfortunately alive and well in search engine marketing. Using black hat SEO, a competitor can harm your site rankings. In a practice sometimes called *Google bowling*, someone else frames your site for link spamming. They generate automated links to bad neighborhoods and make it appear that you're guilty of link spamming. Google then drops your search rankings.

One of the most famous examples of link spamming was a "miserable failure." Thousands of links using "miserable failure" in the anchor text pointed to white house.gov, President George Bush.

When asked about negative SEO, Matt Cutts, a senior software engineer for Google, offered this comment: "Piling links onto a competitor's site to reduce its search ranking isn't impossible, but it's extremely difficult. We try to be mindful of when a technique can be abused and make our algorithm robust against it. I won't go out on a limb and say it's impossible. But Google bowling is much more inviting as an idea than it is in practice." (*The Saboteurs of Search*, Andy Greenberg, Forbes.com, October 2007).

Content Spamming

Content spamming involves tricking a search engine into thinking a website has relevant, keyword-rich content when it really doesn't. Some of these methods create website copy that is not only irrelevant but cumbersome for the website visitor to read. Others show nothing to the visitor, but are still considered black hat. The specific types of content spamming are outlined below.

Keyword stuffing comes in four categories: content keyword stuffing, image keyword stuffing, meta tag keyword stuffing, and invisible text keyword stuffing.

Content Keyword Stuffing

When your content has a keyword density that's higher than 2 to 5 percent, not only does its ridiculousness negatively affect your credibility in the eyes of your visitors, it's also flagged as spam.

Don't confuse legitimate SEO writing with keyword stuffing. More than likely, even if you're an average SEO writer, you won't do keyword stuffing. Writers who do keyword stuffing do it on purpose and know that their content looks crazy. They don't care about their visitors; they just want to rank high in the search engines and hope that the visitor will concentrate more on the banner or link ads than the content. An example of keyword-stuffed content would be as follows:

> *Cheap Laptops.com offers the best in cheap laptops. The cheap laptops available from Cheap Laptops.com are as low as $300! Not only that, but the cheap laptops from Cheap Laptops.com make the cost even cheaper with its free shipping, available for a limited time. Also, the cheap laptops are not cheap when it comes to the brands available. With Cheap Laptops.com, you can buy Sony, Gateway, Dell, Toshiba, Acer, HP and more. Just because Cheap Laptops.com offers cheap laptops doesn't mean that you'll have to settle for generic brands. Indeed, you won't be able to find cheap laptops anywhere else but from Cheap Laptops.com. So come on down and get your cheap laptop today from Cheap Laptops.com. You'll be happy once your brand new cheap laptop from Cheap Laptops.com comes in the mail. On top of that with Cheap Laptops.com you don't have to pay shipping for your cheap laptop. Try getting that from Amazon, eBay or other sites selling cheap laptops. I guarantee you won't be able to find free shipping on cheap laptops at any place other than Cheap Laptops.com.*

See how insane it is? And can you guess the keyword density for that awful content? With as many times as "cheap laptops" appears, you would think the keyword density would be crazy, like 20 percent. But it was only 8 percent, not much higher than what you can legitimately do, which is 5 percent. Don't worry. More than likely, you won't produce such trash because you're not trying to. For comparison purposes, below is an example of appropriate SEO writing:

> *If you're looking for a good deal on laptops, look no further than Cheap Laptops.com. With Cheap Laptops.com, you can buy laptops for as low as $300. Some of the brands that are available include: Sony, Gateway, Dell, Toshiba, Acer, HP and more. Additionally, as an added bonus, the site is offering free shipping for a limited period of time. So, if you're looking to save money on your next laptop purchase, consider visiting Cheap Laptops.com.*

The keyword "cheap laptops" is used only three times, yet since there are only 75 words it still has a keyword density of a healthy 4 percent. This copy is significantly easier to read, and more important, won't get flagged as spam. In the long run, you'll want to stick with this type of copy. The first one may get you a high ranking for a short time, but once search engines catch up to the spam technique, your site will get banned.

It should be noted that there's an even more blatant variant of content keyword stuffing. This form may have legitimate content in the areas of the website that are most likely to be visited (such as at the top or, more commonly, toward the middle of the page), but at the bottom is garbage. It's usually not even in the form of content, but rather a bunch of keywords.

Image Keyword Stuffing

While Google and other search engines can't read images or text that might be on them, they do read what is in the 'alt' attribute (often incorrectly referred to as an image tag), which offers a description of what an image is.

The normal use of the alt tag is to place a one-word description of your image. It can be a keyword *if the keyword relates to the image*. If it doesn't relate, then you should say what it is.

Meta Tag Keyword Stuffing

Keyword stuffing the title tag can cause lots of keywords to show up in the title browser and make the site look unprofessional. Another black hat technique is to spam the keyword and description attribute. It's not uncommon to stuff so many keywords into these attributes that the HTML code is pages long.

Invisible Text Keyword Stuffing

Invisible text is the practice of putting lists of keywords in white text on a white background. This practice gets more spiders to crawl the site. The webmaster makes the text the same color as the background, so it's invisible to the visitor. Regular content would appear in a table or image, so that it's still visible. The hope is that the search engine will index a site that, to the naked eye, looks legitimate.

Gateway or Doorway Pages

Gateway or doorway pages are small web pages that contain a small amount of content and link to a legitimate web page. They used to be considered a white hat SEO tactic, until people started using them strictly for the purpose of tricking spiders to index the site higher.

Wiki Spam

Introduced in the late '90s, wikis are a special kind of site that lets users post and edit websites as they see fit. They're most commonly used for informational purposes, with wikipedia.com being the most popular example. In terms of wiki spam, Wikipedia puts it in five categories: article spam, link spamming, source soliciting, spam bots, and canvassing.

Article Spam

While writing articles about your website can be an excellent white hat SEO tactic, it can become black hat when they're placed on inappropriate websites. Wikis not geared for advertising are an example. If a spam article is found on Wikipedia, it can be deleted with the {{db-spam}} command. A person could also use Wikipedia's proposed deletion option or list it on Wikipedia's "Articles for Deletion" section. However, sometimes Wikipedia leaves the article up to be rewritten in the more encyclopedia-like tone that Wikipedia uses. Note that Wikipedia doesn't discourage articles about companies; they just have to be written properly.

Wiki Link Spamming

In the case of Wikipedia, there are two places where links are allowed: at the end of the article in the list of sources and in the section to the right of the article in a grey box that shows contact information. If a link is listed anywhere else, it's considered spam. If a website is listed in the right place but doesn't relate to what is being talked about, it's still spam.

Source Soliciting

Source soliciting is when webmasters go on "article talk pages" to solicit editors to use their websites. They make the claim that their website could offer more content to an article.

Spam Bots

Spam bots are used to collect e-mails from various websites on the internet or to post spam on various sites. In the case of wiki spam, the spam bots place advertising links on articles they find. The purpose is not advertising, but the hope that search engines see that they have several one-way links from popular web pages.

Canvassing

Canvassing is the process of sending messages to Wikipedians in hopes of starting discussion. It is not considered solicitation because the initial message may not have the tone of an ad. The canvassing techniques used by spammers include friendly notices, cross-posting, campaigning, vote-stacking, and forum shopping.

Page Hijacking

Page hijacking is a black hat technique that can be scary, especially if it's done on sites where people freely give their private information. In this case, the webmaster copies a legitimate website that later redirects visitors to malicious websites. In fact, even the hijacked page itself could be malicious. For example, it could ask for important information such as passwords, Social Security numbers, and credit card information. People give them out because they think they're visiting a legitimate site.

The Consequences of Black Hat SEO

When Google excludes certain pages from appearing in the results pages, they are shown in what Google calls the "supplemental index." Pages in the supplemental index may show up in search results, but pages in the main index are always given priority. With Google being the most powerful search engine, getting into their main index and out of the supplemental index should be one of your top priorities.

There are many reasons why your web page might end up in Google's supplemental index. You may not have enough content on your page to justify putting the page in the main results. Too much duplicate content can also hurt your chances and land you in the supplemental index. Too many query strings in the URL of your site can make finding your page difficult for Google's crawlers.

Also, orphaned pages—pages that aren't linked to any others inside your site—can hurt you. Avoid having the same titles and descriptions on every page, as this can land you in the supplemental index, as well—it can cause problems with the crawlers, as they see just another form of duplicate content.

The linking structure of your website can also get you into the supplemental index. If all you have are reciprocal links with potentially bad neighbors, this increases your chances of getting dumped into the supplemental index. Check to see if a page that no longer exists has an old, cached version of itself in the supplemental listings. That can drag the rest of your site down as well.

Should your website be afflicted by any or all of these problems, fear not. There are ways to get out of the supplemental index and back into the main results. If you're in the supplemental index, you are being crawled. Google does know you're there. But you'll have to take action to get into the main index.

Eliminate all duplicate content issues on your web pages. This is most likely your largest concern and should be dealt with as soon as possible. Google wants every result to be unique, as users get frustrated dealing with the same information page after page. Keep every page on your site as unique as possible. Also, improve the content you already have.

Shorten filenames for static websites, or decrease the number of folders used, as this decreases the complexity of your URL. Give each page a unique and descriptive title, as well. This keeps the crawlers from finding more duplicate content in your pages' titles and descriptions. Simply using the company name or website name on every page won't help the search engines specify the content subjects and topics on each page.

Improve your site architecture. Every page you want to have indexed by search engines should have links to it. Use a sitemap to make sure there's a link to every page. This might not be enough, so make sure you use links throughout the site, whenever relevant. If you have no links to a particular page because you'd like that page not to be found, put that page in your website's "robots.txt" file. This tells the search engine to ignore that page.

Google considers how far a page is from the homepage. Although distance is impossible to avoid with larger websites, a good rule of thumb is that all pages should be accessible from the homepage in two clicks or less. Look for relevant pages that can link together. Use links in the text of articles, and at the end of articles, to related pages. The sitemap also works well here.

Get listed in directories Google trusts. Yahoo!, Open Directory Project, Business.com, Microsoft SBD, and LinkCentre are all good examples. You could start a blog and link to a different inner page every day, or write and submit articles with links to different inner pages. If you trade links with other websites, do so only with relevant, non-spam sites, and encourage them to link to your inner pages. Also, make sure that your content hasn't been stolen, as Google might rank the plagiarized content instead of yours.

If all else fails, there are more drastic measures you can take. You can rename all the pages stranded in the supplemental index and save them as new, with new URLs. Link to these "new" pages prominently on your site, and use a 301 redirect from the old URLs to the new ones. This takes a lot of work if you have a lot of pages in the supplemental index.

Finally, tell Google what's going on. If you feel you've exhausted every option, use the sitemaps to send your URL directly to Google. Also, be patient. Google isn't known for quick responses when webmasters push to have their pages put back into the main results index.

Do not be fooled by the growing subculture of black hat webmasters who use black hat SEO techniques and are proud of it. There are several message boards and even books promoting black hat SEO techniques. There was even one website that talked about the "myths" of white hat versus black hat SEO. Be aware that there are no myths with white hat SEO. White hat SEO is what you're supposed to do. It may take a while to get the results you want, but you have nothing to feel guilty about when you use white hat SEO tactics. You also have nothing to hide because you followed all of the appropriate guidelines when embarking on a SEO campaign.

Source: *Ultimate Guide to Search Engine Optimization: Drive Traffic, Boost Conversion Rates and Make Lots of Money*, Jon Rognerud, (Entrepreneur Press, 2008)

Appendix D
Public Relations Industry Resources

They say you can never be too rich or too thin. While either of these could be argued, we believe you can never have enough resources. Therefore, we're giving you a wealth of sources to check into, check out, and harness for your own personal information blitz.

These sources are tidbits—ideas to get you started on your research. They are by no means the only sources out there, and they should not be taken as the ultimate answer. We have done our research, but businesses do tend to move, change, fold, and expand. As we have repeatedly stressed, do your homework. Get out there and start investigating!

Professional Associations

American Association of Advertising Agencies (AAAA), 405 Lexington Ave., 18th Floor, New York, NY 10174-1801, (212) 682-2500, aaaa.org

Association for Women in Communications, 3337 Duke St., Alexandria, VA 22314, (703) 370-7436, womcom.org

Canadian Public Relations Society, National Office, 4195 Dundas St. West, Suite 346, Toronto, Ontario, M8X 1Y4, Canada, (416) 239-7034, cprs.ca

Council of Public Relations Firms, 317 Madison Ave., Suite 2320, New York, NY 10017, (877) 733-4767, prfirms.org

Direct Marketing Association, 1120 Avenue of the Americas, New York, NY 10036-6700, (212) 768-7277, the-dma.org

Entertainment Publicists Professional Society, PO Box 5841, Beverly Hills, CA 90209-5841, (888) 399-3777, eppsonline.org

Institute for Public Relations, University of Florida, PO Box 118400, Gainesville, FL 32611-8400, (352) 392-0280, instituteforpr.com

International Association of Business Communicators (IABC), One Hallidie Plaza, Suite 600, San Francisco, CA 94102, (415) 544-4700, iabc.com

International Public Relations Association (IPRA), 1 Dunley Hill Court, Ranmore Common, Dorking, Surrey RH5 6SX, United Kingdom, + 44 01483 280 130, ipra.org

Issue Management Council, 207 Loudoun St., SE, Leesburg, VA 20175-3115, (703) 777-8450, issuemanagement.org

National Association of Government Communicators, 201 Park Washington Court, Falls Church, VA 22046-4527, (703) 538-1787, nagc.com

National Investor Relations Institute, 8020 Towers Crescent Dr., Suite 250, Vienna, VA 22182, (703) 506-3570, niri.org

North American Broadcasters Association, PO Box 500, Station A, Toronto, Ontario M5W 1E6, Canada, (416) 598-9877, nabanet.com

Public Relations Society of America (PRSA), 33 Maiden Lane, 11th Floor, New York, NY 10038-5150, (212) 460-1400, prsa.org

Government Agencies and Related Resources

Federal Trade Commission, 600 Pennsylvania Ave. NW, Washington, DC, 20580, (202) 326-2222, ftc.gov

IRS, check your local telephone directory for local offices and phone numbers, irs.gov

Library of Congress, Copyright Office, 101 Independence Ave. SE, Washington, DC 20559-6000, (202) 707-3000, loc.gov/copyright

U.S. Department of Labor, Occupational Safety & Health Administration, 200 Constitution Ave. NW, Room S-1032, Washington, DC 20210, (800) 321-6742, osha.gov

U.S. Department of Labor, Office of Public Affairs, 200 Constitution Ave. NW, Room S-1032, Washington, DC 20210, (202) 219-8211, dol.gov

U.S. Patent and Trademark Office, Washington, DC 20231, (800) 786-9199 or (703) 308-4357, uspto.gov

U.S. Business Advisor, business.gov

U.S. Department of Labor, Bureau of Labor Statistics, bls.gov

Internet Resources

Angry Journalist, angryjournalist.com

Elance, bid on projects or find professionals to work for you, elance.com

HARO"Help a Reporter Out, a daily e-mail list of source requests from journalists, helpareporterout.com

Lingo 2 Word, text messaging terminology, lingo2word.com

OnlinePR, resources and information on PR online, onlinepr.com

ProfNet, connect reporters with experts, profnet.com

Search Engine Watch, search engine marketing tips and news, searchenginewatch.com

Technorati Inc., tracking the world live web, technorati.com

Salary.com, salary.com

Article Sites

Article City, articlecity.com

Article Click, articleclick.com

Article Dashboard, articledashboard.com

Ezine Articles, ezinearticles.com

Get My Articles, getmyarticles.com

Go Articles, goarticles.com

Helium, helium.com

SelfGrowth, selfgrowth.com

Suite 101, suite101.com

Web Know How, webknowhow.net

Web Pro News, webpronews.com

Online Press Release Distribution

Business Wire, businesswire.com

Corporate News, corporatenews.com

eReleases, ereleases.com

Free Press Release, free-press-release.com

News Release Wire, newsreleasewire.com

PR Web Press Release Newswire, prwebdirect.com

Press Release Network, pressreleasenetwork.com

Recommended Reading

Associated Press Stylebook, Basic Books.

The Chicago Manual of Style: The Essential Guide for Writers, Editors, and Publishers, 15th Edition, University of Chicago Press.

The Complete Idiot's Guide to Guerrilla Marketing, Susan Drake and Colleen Wells, Alpha, 2008.

The Entrepreneur's Almanac, Jacquelyn Lynn, Entrepreneur Media, 2007.

Meatball Sundae: Is Your Marketing Out of Sync?, Seth Godin, Portfolio Hardcover, 2007.

The New Rules of Marketing and PR: How to Use News Releases, Blogs, Podcasting, Viral Marketing and Online Media to Reach Buyers Directly, David Meerman Scott, Wiley, 2007.

Miscellaneous Resources

Bill Stoller's PublicityInsider.com, publicityinsider.com

Carbonite, online backup, carbonite.com

Copyblogger, Brian Clark, copywriting tips for online marketing, copyblogger.com

KDPaine's PR measurement blog, PR research and evaluation, kdpaine.blogs.com/

Liseydreams Web and Graphic Design, Elise Cronin-Hurley, PO Box 1394, Winter Park, FL 32790, liseydreams.com

The Publicity Hound, Joan Stewart, tips for free publicity, 3434 County KK, Port Washington, WI 53074, (262) 284-7451, publicityhound.com

Web Ink Now, online thought leadership and viral marketing strategies using blogs, news releases, ebooks, and online media, webinknow.com

Public Relations Firms

Annie Jennings PR, publicist for authors and speakers, book promotion, (908) 281-6201, anniejenningspr.com

EnTech Public Relations, Kate Kaemerle, (206) 854-1488, entechpr.com

Bernstein Crisis Management Inc., Jonathan Bernstein, 180 S. Mountain Trail, Sierra Madre, CA 91024, (626) 825-3838, bernsteincrisismanagement.com

Sanderson & Associates, Rhonda Sanderson, 1052 West Fulton Market St., 3W, Chicago, IL 60607, (312) 829-4350, sandersonpr.com

Media Relations Inc., 350 West Burnsville Parkway, Suite 350, Burnsville, MN 55337, (612) 798-7200, publicity.com

Publicity Guaranteed, publicityguaranteed.com

Development Counsellors International Inc., 215 Park Ave., S., 10th Floor, New York, NY 10003, (212) 725-0707, theleaderinmarketingplaces.com

LaunchSquad, 611 Mission St., 7th Floor, San Francisco, CA 94105, (415) 625-8555, launchsquad.com

Perkett PR Inc., 34 Cohasset Ave., Marshfield, MA 02050, (781) 834-5852, perkettpr.com

Glossary

Advertising: material designed to promote a product, idea, or service presented to the public by means of paid space or broadcast time.

Advocacy journalism: a type of journalism that intentionally and transparently adopts a nonobjective viewpoint, usually for some social or political purpose.

Alternative media: the communication media that are alternatives to mainstream media.

Angle: the particular approach a reporter takes in writing a story.

Backgrounder: a briefing or report intended only for the purpose of providing background information to the media.

Beat: in journalism, the area regularly covered by a reporter.

Blog: a weblog.

Byline: the name of the writer positioned under the headline at the beginning of an article.

Bylined article: refers to an article written and submitted for publication by a nonmedia person, usually an expert in a particular field; bylined articles may be ghostwritten.

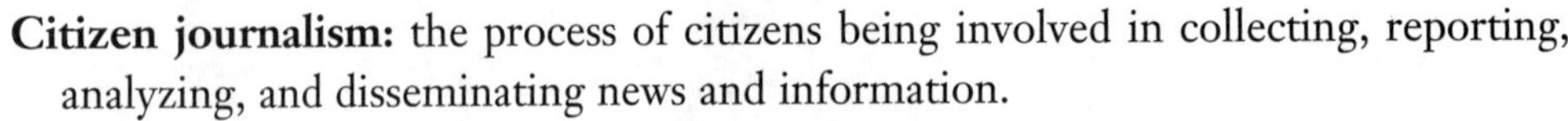

Citizen journalism: the process of citizens being involved in collecting, reporting, analyzing, and disseminating news and information.

Columnist: a writer of a column in a publication, such as a newspaper or magazine.

Community journalism: locally oriented media coverage that focuses on city neighborhoods or individual suburbs.

Copy: written text.

Defamation: the expression of injurious, malicious statements about a person or entity.

Dynamic content: information in websites that changes automatically based on database or user information.

Embargo date: a heading on a news release indicating that the news is not to be reported before that date.

Exclusive: an interview or story opportunity presented solely to one reporter or publication and not to others.

Fact sheet: a list of facts or statistics about a particular topic that allows media to quickly grasp a particular issue or situation.

Fourth estate: a term describing journalists and journalism in general.

Ghostwriting: writing generated without published credit to its author and often credited to another.

Gonzo journalism: a type of journalism that blends fact and fiction with subjective writing and the reporter often being part of the story.

Graf: paragraph.

Investigative journalism: a type of journalism in which reporters deeply investigate an incident or issue that involves a crime, corruption, or scandal.

Journalist: a person who gathers and disseminates news and information.

Keyword: a word or words that can be searched for in documents or menus.

Lead story: article that is given primary attention and prominent placement on the first page of a publication, or the first story on a news broadcast.

Lead: the beginning of a news story, generally containing the five Ws: who, what, when, where, and why.

Literary journalism: a type of journalism that uses literary styles and techniques to tell a factually accurate story.

Mainstream media: traditional media including television, newspapers, and radio that reach a wide audience, usually owned and controlled by big corporations and/or government.

Marketing PR: using press releases on the internet as a marketing tool.

Mash-up media: a media content technique formed by merging two or more sets of data.

Media call report: a log recording those media that were sent a release or contacted for a specific pitch, which details when the contact was made, with whom, and to what result.

Microsite (minisite, weblet): a web page or cluster of pages meant to function as an auxiliary supplement to a primary website.

Mobile marketing: marketing on or with a mobile device or unit.

News: new information of any kind.

Newsworthy: information of sufficient interest or importance to the public to warrant reporting in the media.

Official statement: a written comment prepared for the purpose of responding consistently to any question from the media regarding a particular controversial issue.

Opinion journalism: a type of journalism that features a subjective viewpoint, usually with some social or political purpose.

Podcast: collection of digital media files distributed over the internet for playback on personal computers and portable media players.

Press conference (news conference): an event where journalists are invited to hear a presentation and then are usually offered the opportunity to ask questions.

Press kit (media kit): a package of background materials in either printed or electronic format detailing various aspects of an organization that is presented to members of the media.

Press release (media release): an announcement of an event, information, or other newsworthy item issued to the press.

Product launch: the introduction of a new product to the market.

Publication of information material: making information known to the public at large through off- or online means.

Reporter: a writer, investigator, or presenter of news stories.

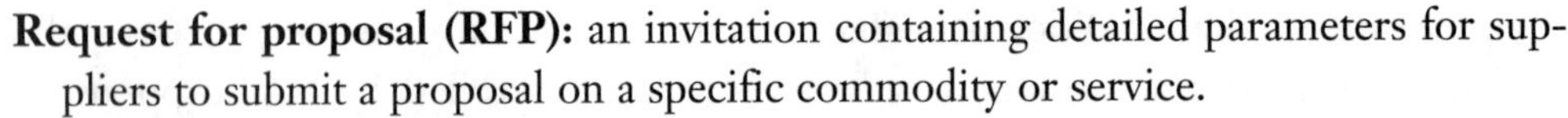

Request for proposal (RFP): an invitation containing detailed parameters for suppliers to submit a proposal on a specific commodity or service.

RSS: really simple syndication.

Satellite feed: broadcast material sent via a satellite that is orbiting the earth.

Search engine optimization (SEO): the practice of designing web pages so they rank as high as possible in search results from search engines.

Search engine: software that searches for information and returns sites that provide that information.

Seminars: training events typically targeted to a company's customers or potential customers.

Special events: events designed to generate publicity and public interest.

Speeches: presentations that provide public and media exposure for the speaker and organization.

Spider (crawler): software that visits websites and indexes the pages on those sites.

Spin: a sometimes pejorative term signifying a heavily biased portrayal in one's own favor of an event or situation.

Video news release (VNR): video segments designed to look like news reports that are distributed to television newsrooms and incorporated into newscasts.

Watchdog journalism: a type of journalism that seeks to hold various public personalities and institutions accountable for their actions.

Webcast: a live or recorded broadcast of an event over the internet.

Wire service distribution: a wire service is a news-gathering organization that distributes syndicated copy electronically; distribution by wire service is an alternative to traditional news release distribution methods of regular mail and fax.

Index

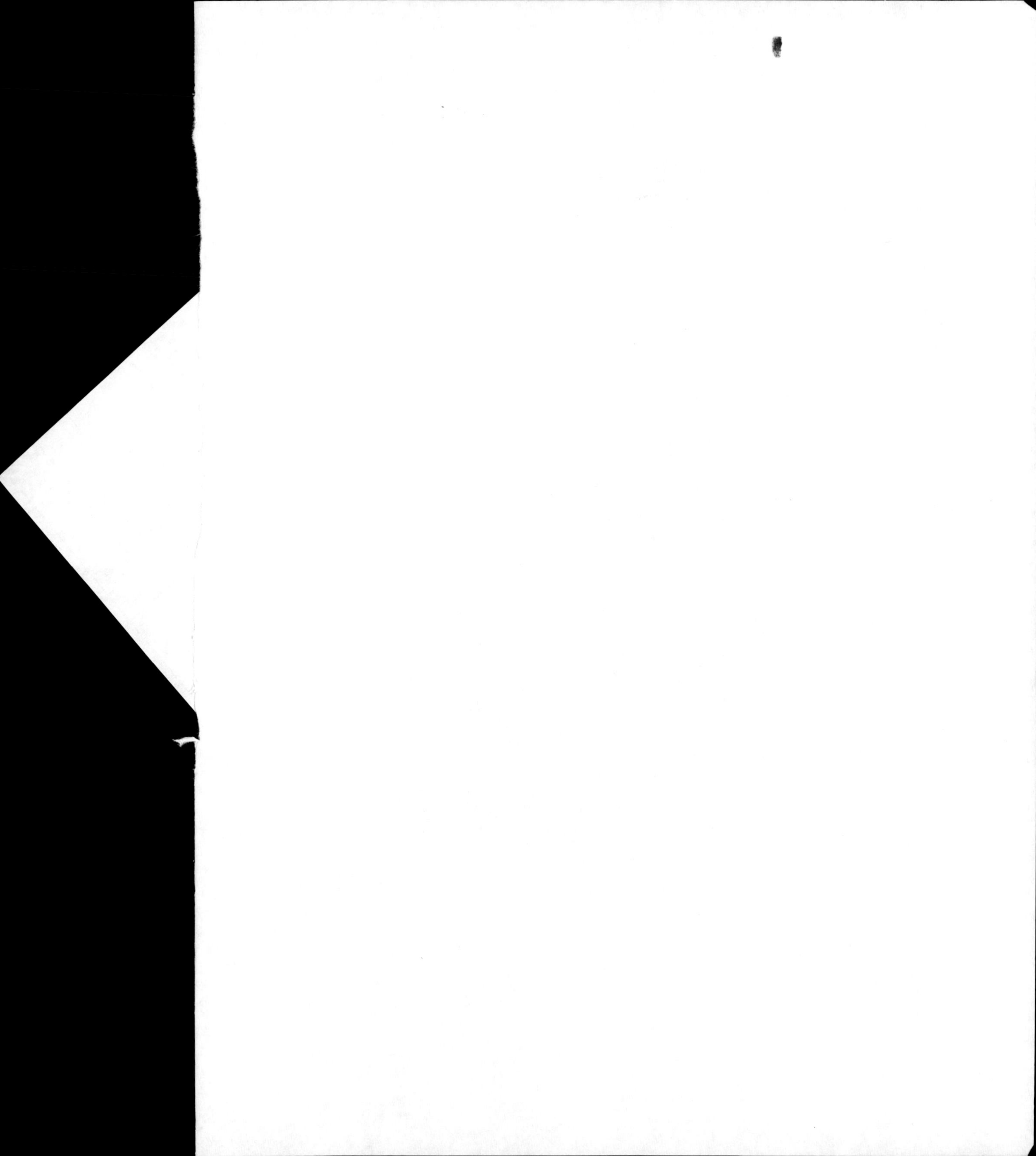